Copyright ©2011 by Steve Cohn
First Edition

All rights reserved. No part of this book shall be reproduced, stored in a retrieval system, or transmitted by any means without written permission from the author.

Published by People to People Learning, Inc.
560 Summer Breeze Court
Alpharetta, GA 30005
770-667-3042
www.PeopleToPeopleLearning.com

ISBN 978-0-9827598-0-6
Library of Congress Control Number: 2011932207
Printed in the United States of America

Cover Design by Elizabeth Bell, eBELLDesign
Back Cover Photo by Hannah J. Cohn

The following are registered trademarks referenced:
Air Jamaica, American Express, Apple, Arizona Diamondbacks, Associated Press, AT&T, Atlanta Braves, Bank of America, Best Buy, Burger King, Carmine's, Chevrolet, CMO Council, Coca-Cola, Coke, Coke Zero, Crazy Eddie, Creating CEOs, Customer Focus Inc., Dell, Delta Air Lines, Diet Coke, Disney, Facebook, Farmer's Insurance, Google, hhgregg, iPhone, JD Power and Associates, Land's End, Lexus, Marriott, McDonald's, Microsoft, National Speakers Association (NSA), NSA Georgia, New York Mets, New York Yankees, Nordstrom's, PBS, Ponderosa Steakhouse, PowerPoint, Publix Supermarkets, Sabermetrix, Southwest Airlines, Starbucks, Strativity Group, Taylor Guitars, Tiffany, Toastmasters, Twitter, United Airlines, United Continental, UPS, Visa, Walmart, Wegman's Supermarkets, Wendy's, YouTube

What People Are Saying About *It's Not Rocket Service*

"Steve Cohn has managed to simplify a seemingly complex process (customer support) into an entertaining and illuminating series of stories and frameworks in his book *It's Not Rocket Service* ... and he's spot on!

Customer service technology providers, trainers, consultants, so-called 'experts,' and many practitioners make it too difficult for their front-line staff and, more depressingly (as I described in my 1st book *The Best Service is No Service*) for their customers. Using personal stories, a wealth of consulting and seminar experiences and other citations, Steve argues persuasively how concepts such as 'silence is lethal,' 'is the customer always right?', 'not all customers are created equal,' 'red rules' and 'blue rules' can simplify interactions, and offers many other insights.

Starting with probing questions on 'what do your customers expect?' of your service operations, Steve proceeds to strip back unnecessary processes and focus squarely on the moments of truth; the face-to-face or customer service representative connections. 'Connection' is key to Steve's persuasive premise: we need to connect with our customers, our co-workers, and each other; connect in a meaningful, listening way. When we do that – when customer service does that right, then 'it's not rocket service' and companies, their staff, and most importantly their customers benefit.

Read *It's Not Rocket Service* to find solid examples of how to build great service experiences, learn from bad stories, and realize how few times you've personally had the right type of service."

BILL PRICE, President, Driva Solutions and
Co-author of *The Best Service is No Service*

"*It's Not Rocket Service* is a brilliant book, ready to transform the entire world of customer service. Steve Cohn has put together a program that takes off with a simple philosophy: make customer service a priority – from the top – and nurture it at every level of the organization, never losing focus.

Don't you love the sound of 'rocket service?' This simple term illustrates how powerful Steve's concept is and how, once it takes off with sufficient fuel (continued training), then the sales stay high and the profits remain respectable, if not superlative.

As Steve points out, it's not that the customer is always right, because we know he or she is sometimes shortsighted or at least narrow in perspective. No, it's that the customer needs to feel right and it's our task to make that happen if we want the business. So train your associates to make the customer feel right – by observing and supporting the process. It doesn't happen by itself and, in large organizations, service can easily fall between the cracks.

Steve says 'It's not about you,' and in that simple statement, he reveals the crisp, underlying philosophy of this powerful approach: when expectations are exceeded, then the customer comes back with an open wallet. And it's so easy to exceed expectations merely by fine tuning our personal interactions to make the customer feel like a king or queen. It doesn't take more money or goods or time. Just think with a smile and an open, supportive mind when dealing with the customer. Make 'em feel they're right! It's that simple.

Steve Cohn's *It's Not Rocket Service* gets you on target. When you fully understand his underlying structure – with the necessary, effective principles of interaction that make it simple, your business will take off. Ready? Three, two, one …"

Dr. David Ryback
Author of *ConnectAbility*, *Dreams That Come True*,
and *Putting Emotional Intelligence to Work*

"*It's Not Rocket Service* is the most insightful and at the same time, very practical book on Customer Service since the eighties! What I like most about the book is its emphasis on customer conversations as a great enabler of customer experience."

    JAGDISH N. SHETH, Charles H. Kellstadt Professor of Marketing, Goizueta Business School, Emory University, Author of *Clients for Life*

"*It's Not Rocket Service* really resonates with professionals who work in the area of customer service and customer support. I found Steve's work to be meaningful in today's competitive landscape, insightful, and practical. The concepts are complex but the reading is simple and enjoyable. In our world of commodities and instant information Steve reminds us that people still do business with people and those who do that best win every time!!"

    DAVID A. DAFFNER, Vice President of Operations, Curtis1000 Inc.

"Drawing on years of experience advising hundreds of companies, Steve Cohn delivers a clear and easy to follow platform for customer service excellence. Now it is your choice. Are you ready to embrace your customers? If yes, read this book and share it with all your employees. Delight your customers and profit."

    LIOR ARUSSY, President, Strativity Group and Author of *Customer Experience Strategy* (2010)

"For busy people with an interest in improving customer service, this is a fast read – clear and to the point with relevant examples. I especially enjoyed Steve's personal anecdotes and stories which made the concepts real. I have the utmost confidence that if you put into practice the ideas in this book, you will see great results!"

    PAMELA COLLINS, RN MSN MS FACHE, Vice-President, Chief Patient Services Officer McCullough-Hyde Memorial Hospital

"*It's Not Rocket Service* is appropriately titled. Steve Cohn provides a real world analysis of what's right and what's wrong with customer service today. His suggestions and insights provide anyone a simple but effective course of action for delivering superior service."

    MARK SANBORN, President of Sanborn & Associates, Inc. and Author of *The Fred Factor & You Don't Need a Title to be a Leader*

"Steve Cohn gets customer service. *It's Not Rocket Service* packages sophisticated, powerful and unique customer service concepts into a simple, understandable program. The impact of this book and his work will exceed your expectations!"

ELIZABETH B. WALDEN, Executive Director
University of Louisville Health Care Outpatient Center

"*It's Not Rocket Service* shows that customer service need not be difficult or complicated. Through this book, Steve Cohn will help you and your people become more successful by providing the personal touch in all internal and external interactions as well as in managing your employees. We have used Steve's ideas in our business. Read this book to find out how to use them in yours."

LARRY M. DAVIDSON
CEO, First American Home Buyers Protection Corp.

"Steve totally changed our philosophy and attitude in servicing our customers and even changed the way we deal with people in our personal life. Now you have a chance to learn what we learned and make your customers happy too."

ETTY OZIR-BEREZIN
After Sale Service Manager, Raymond Weil USA

"A poignant reminder of an important business fundamental. Building a solid and loyal customer base is an essential component for success, and this book will put you in the right mindset to hone that craft."

DR. NIDO QUBEIN, President, High Point University, and Chairman, Great Harvest Bread Co.

"What a blast! *It's Not Rocket Service*, by Steve Cohn, is an innovative approach to growing your business by getting your people to understand, manage, and exceed customer expectations."

STEPHEN TWEED, Chairman and CEO, Leading Home Care

"This book breaks down customer service into actionable steps which any company can put into action creating repeat business. Creating a positive customer experience is simple and you really don't have to be a rocket scientist to understand it."

KRISTIN KELLY, Rocket Scientist

IT'S NOT ROCKET SERVICE

Managing, Meeting & Exceeding Customer Expectations

By Steve Cohn

*For my Father and my Grandfather,
who taught me the value of serving customers*

Courtesy of www.Brooklynpix.com

Dad (highlighted on left) and Grandpa Max (highlighted on right)
outside Mac's Men's Shop during a parade

With Gratitude

A book is never the result of one person's work. Quite a few people were instrumental in making this book a reality through their contributions, thoughts, support, information, and encouragement. I thank them all from the bottom of my heart.

My wife and soul mate, Arlene gave me the space, the belief and the encouragement to pursue this dream. She has been my biggest fan and stood with me every step of the way, even when I didn't deserve it. She allowed me to "wander" the world to collect the stories and ideas that make up this book. She's also been knee-deep in this project from proof reading the first draft of the manuscript to creating the book's layout.

My children, Ariel and Hannah have been a great audience for my customer service stories all these years. Now they'll be able to read them to their children one day. They lifted my highest highs and lightened my darkest lows by looking at me as if I were the "coolest" Dad in the world.

My Mom was prescient and inspiring when she told me long ago that she gave me the middle name "Norman" so I could use "Steve Norman" as my pen name. I didn't use the pen name, but she planted the seed in my mind to become an author. My brothers David and Ted and all of my family members have been my most dependable supporters, and they've listened to me when I went on and on about great and terrible customer service.

My Dad and my Grandpa Max, as I said in the dedication, taught me the value of serving customers. I didn't realize it at the time, but Mac's Men's Shop was a laboratory where I first tried out my customer service skills.

Steve Fugate has been a true friend, mentor and sounding board. His advice and wisdom helped me move from being a customer service trainer and seminar leader to being a true consultant. Dr. Richard Strand of Customer Focus, Inc. got me started in customer service training with his wonderful course, *Creating CEOs* (Customer Experience Owners) and was the first to teach me many of the concepts in this book. Sheila Billingsley and Kathy Biagi hired and collaborated with me in taking clients to another level of customer relationships, as well as shared countless good times and lots of laughs. The rest of the Customer Focus team has supported me, kept me working and have been true partners throughout these past 15 years.

Lior Arussy, Rachel Yurowitz. Michael Starr and the Strativity Group expanded my consciousness of true customer experience in so many ways, showing me how the customer experience is so much more than soft skills. Lior's perspectives have colored my perspectives in more ways than I can count.

Elizabeth Bell beautifully designed the cover. She brilliantly captured the concepts, content and style of the book and turned it into art. Jennifer Scoggins superbly edited an editor who could no longer see what was good, bad, confusing, overwrought, funny, important, and right about his manuscript. She made this book better than I ever could have myself.

Rachel Yurowitz, Sharon Guttman, David Daffner, Dr. Chuck Sodikoff, Bart Segal, Dr. David Ryback, and Sheila Billingsley were my second set of eyes and gave me great feedback after I thought the manuscript was done. They asked me tough questions and made me reexamine my perceptions, opinions, and content until I was sure of them. The book is twice as good as it was originally because of their suggestions.

Sam Horn helped me form an outline for what this book has become and came up with the title, *It's Not Rocket Service*. My childhood friend, Brian Merlis, of BrooklynPix, provided the photograph of Mac's Men's Shop in the dedication.

Dr. David Ryback, Jean Houston Shore, Bill Kovach, Paul Johnson, and Jim Dawson provided me with professional advice, wisdom, friendship and caring through good times and bad. Dick Biggs, Alan Black, Ken Futch, Jim Hunt, Mark Mayberry, Austin McGonigle,

Doug Smart and Mike Stewart were indispensible mentors and friends who helped pave the way for me to bring these concepts to the world.

Thousands of clients, class participants and audience members let me touch their lives and share what I know and love. They challenged me and gave me the real-life examples that you'll find throughout this book.

I couldn't have written this book or become a successful speaking professional without the National Speakers Association and my Speakers Roundtable Advanced Toastmasters Club. To my many NSA and Toastmasters friends, too many to mention personally, if you've helped me, mentored me, supported me, taught me, worked with me or shared a laugh or a song, I thank you.

I'd always thought Kay du Pont would be around for me to give her the first signed copy of my book, but it was not meant to be. She took a chance on me a long time ago and put me on the road to the pages that follow. I hope I rewarded her faith in me.

Table of Contents

What People Are Saying About *It's Not Rocket Service* iii

With Gratitude xi

Introduction: It's Not Rocket Service 1

COUNTDOWN:

   10: Start With a Sturdy Launch Pad 11

   9: It's Not About You 33

   8: Expectations Drive Everything 41

   7: R-E-S-P-E-C-T 65

   6: Helplessness is Your Customer's Fuse 81

   5: Name that Problem 111

   4: Be a Customer Advocate 129

   3: Explain Yourself 145

   2: E-Versations 167

   1: Exceeding Expectations is Easy 183

We Have Lift-Off! 201

Notes 213

About Steve Cohn 217

Want More? 219

Index 223

Introduction

It's Not Rocket Service

During the Great Recession of 2009, restaurants all over the country were closing left and right. People cut back on and even stopped eating out altogether because of the bad economy. Yet at the end of the year, as the surviving restaurants were contemplating whether 2010 would be the same, Carmine's Italian restaurant in Alpharetta, GA was preparing to move into a larger space because it couldn't fit all of its customers in its current location.

Two weeks after Carmine's moved to the new location in the same strip mall (where another restaurant had failed to survive), there was still a wait for tables, despite having filled almost double the space. Carmine's not only held onto its old customers, but the restaurant was also becoming the place to go for new customers.

What is it about Carmine's that helped it survive in both a bad economy and a bad business sector and still thrive, attracting more customers than before?

The pizza, the Italian entrees and the prices are very good. But something else brings people into Carmine's over and over again.

I have a unique perspective on Carmine's because my family lives there, or so it seems. We eat at Carmine's at least once a week. When we tell our kids we're going out to eat, the assumption is we're going to Carmine's. We like it that much. Apparently, many other people do, too. Chad Mackes, Carmine's owner, has created an atmosphere that says "Welcome to our home." But Chad doesn't need to tell you this in his marketing; you feel as if they've been serving you your whole life from the minute you sit down. We're regulars but we've heard newcomers say the same thing. When the more experienced servers take our order, they know what drinks we like and note when one of our kids is not with us.

I'm a Coke Zero fanatic. At Carmine's, I always had to order by the bottle because it wasn't in the fountain dispenser. When the new location opened, the server told me with excitement, "Oh! We now have Coke Zero on the fountain, so you can get all the refills you want!" I think she was more excited than I was. (Weeks later, when I saw Chad, he commented that he thought of me when the Coca-Cola salesperson told him he could add Coke Zero to the dispenser.)

When a new server takes our order, he or she treats us the same way. I wouldn't be surprised if some of the more experienced servers see us sit down at a table and fill in the new server on our preferences. Should you bring a couple of friends to Carmine's, the attitude seems to be "Any friend of a customer is a friend of ours!" Unbelievable.

Somebody once told me that the reason why the restaurant industry has so many business failures is because the people who spend the most time with the customers are the lowest paid and most poorly trained people on staff – the servers. Chad has very high standards for his staff. He has high standards for whom he hires and even more so, he has high standards for who he keeps on staff. He's never said so, but I feel as though he tries to emulate the theme song from the old TV show *Cheers* – "You wanna go where everybody knows your name."

It doesn't take a rocket scientist to understand why Carmine's is so successful. A 10-year-old can figure it out. It's the way they make you feel when you're there.

It's not hard to create such an atmosphere for your customers, even if you're not running a restaurant.

It's not rocket service.

Why *It's Not Rocket Service*

I've called this book *It's Not Rocket Service* because I've been helping companies and organizations create great experiences for their customers for years. It continually amazes me how easy it is to produce outstanding customer service yet how few companies and people really get it. They aren't able to institute it in their organizations or even do it well when interacting with customers, but they can tell you – in detail – how some other company, store, restaurant, or business totally screws up the customer experience. I know this because almost every time I tell people I teach customer service for a living, they say, "You teach customer service? Oh, have I got a story for you!"

As people say, "it's not rocket science" to describe something that you don't need to be a genius to understand, I say, "It's not rocket service." "It's not rocket service" says giving great customer service and creating customer loyalty is not difficult and doesn't take an expert to do it well (I actually worked with some rocket scientists and their customer skills were *terrible*).

It's not about where you were born or how you were raised. It doesn't matter if you work in retail, call centers, corporate, supply chains, education, information technology, manufacturing, media, a large company, a small company, or a high-end or fast food restaurant. It doesn't matter if you are a clerk or a CEO, a receptionist or a manager, an employee or an entrepreneur. It doesn't matter if you're an introvert or an extrovert.

You can be great with customers. You can be great with your co-workers. You can be great with people.

If you're a manager, your people can be great at customer service. You can create an environment where your people feel empowered, customer-centric, and willing and able to do what it takes to create long-lasting, passionate customer relationships. It's not difficult.

It's not rocket service.

How Important is the Customer Experience?

The plane was still at the gate and the flight attendant had closed the doors. I was in first class, having been upgraded on a less-than-full flight. Across the aisle from me was a male passenger and next to him was an empty seat.

The passenger called over the flight attendant and asked, "Would you mind if my wife, who is sitting in coach, could sit in this empty seat and join me in first class?" (I know; how did his wife let him get away with sitting in first class while she sat in coach?) The flight attendant took a moment to ponder her next move.

This was what we in the customer experience world call a "moment of truth." In that moment, this one flight attendant's decision would make the difference between a customer's great experience and a normal, mediocre one. She would need to decide whether to love procedure or love the customer. She would create a memorable moment or a forgotten one.

The doors to the plane were closed. There would be no more passengers. The seat would remain empty the entire flight. She could leave it empty, or she could allow the man's wife to come up front.

But there were rules to consider. First class seats are expensive and those that the airline gives away are only for higher-level frequent fliers. How would the other passengers feel if she gave away a seat they had to earn or pay for? Did she have the authority to make such a decision? Would she have to call in to the gate supervisor? What if she made the wrong decision? What would happen then?

It actually took her less than 10 seconds to say, "Sure, why not." The man excitedly started to go to the coach section when the flight attendant said, "You sit here. I'll get her." The excited spouse came up front with a smile from ear to ear, matched only by the smile on her husband's face. The rest of us in first class were smiling, too.

One flight attendant, one moment of truth, one airline's reputation on the line. She could have chosen to follow the rules and the procedures or create a memorable experience. She chose the latter, and now this story about a flight attendant at Delta Air Lines is in a book.

The customer experience is in our hands. Each one of us can make or break the company's future just by creating a great or poor customer experience. The statistics consistently tell us that great customer experiences are a leading driver of customer happiness and loyalty. And much of that experience comes from how the human being handling the situation takes care of the customer.

But is the customer experience really that important? I've been asked this question numerous times by audiences and clients who tell me with all honesty that customers only care about price – the ability to do business and compare prices over the internet has changed the way people purchase forever. This is especially true when I talk to Business-to-Business audiences.

But the facts say otherwise.

Year after year, study after study shows that consumers and businesses will go out of their way to do business with companies and stores that give them outstanding experiences. The *2010 Customer Experience Consumer Study* from Strativity Group, Inc. shows that "consumers notice and financially reward companies that deliver superior customer experience." The survey of consumers in the United States and Canada revealed:

- 73% of consumers stated that they would expand their purchases with a vendor by 10% or more if the customer experience was superior.
- 55% of consumers agreed that they would stay with a vendor for 10 years or more as long as the experience was superior.
- 58% said they would recommend companies that deliver superior customer experiences to others.
- 44% of consumers would be willing to pay a premium price of 5% or more for a superior customer experience.

In another study, the *2010 American Express Global Customer Service Barometer*, Americans said they will spend 9% more with companies that provide excellent service. Also:

- 81% are more likely to repeat business after a good service experience and 52% will never do business with a company again after a poor experience.
- 91% of Americans base their decision to do business with a company on its level of customer service.

Let's look at that last number again. 91%. It's almost an unbelievable number. More than 9 out of 10 people said they do this. Have you ever asked yourself why a certain customer or client left you? Or why you feel your company can't compete in a "commoditized" business sector? Remember that statistic – 91% of Americans base their decision to do business with a company on its level of customer service.

These numbers aren't secret. You can find them just by doing a search on Google. The companies we buy and seek service from have seen them and more than likely have taken their own customer surveys. You would think that in the face of such surveys and with a shaky economy affecting their bottom lines, companies would be kicking the commitment to customer service into high gear. But they're not.

Only 37% of respondents to the American Express survey said that companies had increased their focus on providing quality service and even fewer said companies were changing their customer service attitudes at all. One in five people felt companies take them for granted.

Of course, they could have been talking about all those other companies and not yours. And your customers may be in that 9% who didn't say they base their buying decisions on customer service. How much of a gambler do you have to be to believe this?

It comes down to the company's attitude towards its customers and how the human being who touches the customer demonstrates that attitude.

MORE IMPORTANT THAN SALES?

As somebody who offers customer service/experience seminars, it always puzzles me why companies and people would spend gobs of money on sales training but not on the people who take care of the customers after the sale. The companies always consider the "customer service" department as a non-revenue generating necessity.

It's not. Actually, it may be more important to the bottom line than sales.

Think of it this way: sales and marketing help customers make the decision to buy in the first place. Customer service and all of those who serve your customers help customers make the decision to buy more. While it can be difficult to convince somebody to try your product or store, what's even more difficult is getting them to buy again and again. And if they keep buying again and again, those customers are much more valuable to your business than those who buy only once. *It's not rocket service* to know that you want more of those customers.

Have you ever seen what happens when a salesperson nabs a huge account? What a celebration! Juan (or Juanita) gets slaps on the back, congratulations from the boss, maybe even a little bonus gift for his efforts. His name goes up on the sales chart and everybody knows he's DA MAN!

During the next year or two, the client contacts the company several times for situations big and small and receives remarkable service from Morgan, Noah, Sandie, Jonah and the rest of the underpaid but conscientious customer care or help desk people. The client is *very* happy. At the end of his two-year commitment, he calls to renew the contract.

Odds are there is no celebration in the help desk area. Tracy, the customer service manager, doesn't get a slap on the back, congratulations from the boss, nor does she receive a little bonus. If Tracy doesn't get these things, what do you think Morgan, Noah,

Sandie and Jonah get? Nobody in customer service gets the credit and what's worse, the salesperson gets the huge commission on the renewal and the additional agreements the client signs because he's so happy.

Do these customer care people deserve to get more? Yes, because in the long run, they can affect the bottom line more than sales can. Remember, the Strativity Group study showed that "loyal customers who enjoyed exceptional customer experience are almost three times as likely to continue doing business with companies for another ten years or more than dissatisfied customers."

Which is more profitable, the initial sale or the ongoing business based on customer experience?

There is no doubt that sales are the main driver of company revenue – if customers don't buy your product the first time, they can't experience your company's service. But that sale only gets them in the door; the service area that takes care of the customer after the sale causes the money to keep rolling in.

The next time one of your customers renews an agreement, makes a repeat purchase, or buys additional products and services, I expect a celebration in the customer service department. I'll bring the cake.

What You'll Learn

My goal in this book is to help you and your organization make a commitment to outstanding customer experiences.

Some of what I'll cover includes:

- How the customer experience begins at the top and makes its way through the organization to the people who have direct contact with the customer, not the other way around.

- How customer interactions are never about you and always about the customer. If you make it about them, they'll make it about you.

- Why customer expectations dictate how customers feel about you and your company before, during and after a customer interaction.
- How treating customers as more than just account numbers, demographics or the sum total of their purchases will make them feel closer to you and happier about continuing to do business with your company.
- That there is only one reason customers become upset and how addressing that reason early in the conversation can help avoid conflict and dissatisfaction later on down the road.
- How empathy and apologies go a long way towards creating ongoing customer relationships.
- Why asking questions in the right way can diffuse angry situations, help you solve customer problems quickly and thoroughly, and increase your ability to say "yes" when the answer is usually "no."
- How to become a "Customer Service Hero" and advocate for the customer without hurting the company.
- How to explain clearly and simply and know when to follow or bend the rules.
- How to deal with customers when they don't like your answer.
- How to communicate electronically in a personal, connected and effective way.
- How to "own" the customer's experience and exceed expectations.

I will talk about but not focus on organizational development, using Customer Relationship Management (CRM) technology and the structural steps needed to create a truly customer-centric organization. This book is about people – your customers – and the people who serve them through telephone, face-to-face, and electronic interactions.

TIPS AND TECHNIQUES

Throughout this book, I will provide tips and techniques I've learned from working with and observing employees and management at more than 150 companies throughout the U.S. and internationally. I'll tell stories I've heard, situations I've experienced, and lessons I've taught. Some of the stories will surely seem familiar because I've discovered that most people have similar service experiences.

I've written the book as if I'm talking to you, the reader, in front of a classroom, in an auditorium or even face-to-face in a conversation. I have not intended this book to be a scholarly work. You don't have to be a college professor (or a rocket scientist) to understand it. *It's not rocket service.* Where I mention something somebody taught me or I heard, I have attributed these statements and items to them. You will not find a large section of footnotes.

At the end of each chapter, I will review the most important points (Rocket Review) and share some ideas for managers and supervisors (Manager Lift-Off) on the best ways to institute what I discussed in the chapter. By the time you finish this book, you will have the tools to use your skills to help transform your organization, starting with your own attitudes and actions. The skills you learn will create gratifying and long-lasting personal relationships with customers, co-workers and even friends and family.

It's not rocket service. But what you learn can launch your customer relationships into the stratosphere.

The best compliment I ever received at one of my seminars was "You were very entertaining and so funny, but I never for a moment doubted you were dead serious about great customer service." I hope you feel the same way after you read this book.

Commence countdown!

COUNTDOWN:

Start With a Sturdy Launch Pad

I was negotiating with an Operations Director who wanted me to present my customer service seminar at his company. We had come to a point where we were still somewhat far apart on price and neither side wanted to move. The Operations Director tried to break the deadlock.

"I'll tell you what. I'll pay you the amount I've offered you. If our customer satisfaction ratings go up from 2 to 4 (on a scale of 5) after six months, I'll bring it up to your asking price as a bonus."

"I don't work for incentives," I replied.

"Don't you guarantee your work? If you're as good as you say you are, you should be happy to accept my offer," he answered.

"Oh, I guarantee *my* work. I just can't guarantee yours," I countered. He seemed taken aback by my comment, so I explained further.

"I can guarantee that I will be effective in the session. I will guarantee that your people who take the class will walk out with great skills and a major change in their thinking about customers. However, that's only part of what causes customers to give you higher or lower scores. If your repair people don't fix things properly, I can't control that. If your deliveries to the stores are consistently late,

I can't control that either. I can make your people better, but if your systems are rotten, nothing will help."

He gave in.

It Starts at the Top

This interaction is far too typical of a belief system that many organizations have towards the customer experience: if the customer is unhappy, it's up to the customer service department to fix it. Never mind that the problem or the beginning of the problem took place somewhere else in the organization; the ball is in customer service's court.

Then, these often lower-paid employees are asked to do the impossible without the authority to do what needs to be done. They're given scripts to use when talking to customers, which communicates to the employees that we don't trust them to handle the situation properly and tells the customer that the employees can't think for themselves. We reward them or punish them for how well or poorly they do on metrics that have little to do with the customer experience and everything to do with time and efficiency. Systems are often created that hamper the customer and product experience and affect the ability of the Customer Service Representative (CSR) to do the job he is there to do.

The customer doesn't care how efficient your call center is. She cares whether her problem is being fixed or if the customer service representative can provide the information she needs.

The Launch Pad

Rocket scientists know that you can't launch a rocket without a launch pad to launch it from. Without a foundation to stand on, the rocket can't blast off into space. The customer environment – our attitudes towards the customer/company/employee balance is the foundation on which our customer relationships begin. And you can't launch a customer-centric culture without it.

This chapter is about the customer environment within your company and your department. While much of the book is geared toward managing the interaction between the customer and the company representative (CSR or otherwise), the problems in the customer's situation started somewhere else.

The interaction between the employee and the customer is one of the most important parts of the customer/company dynamic, but it only resolves the problem and avoids customer disappointment. The processes and procedures, the attitude of managers toward employees, and so many other internal issues will strongly affect whether there needs to be an interaction at all.

Much of this chapter is aimed at leaders and managers, but non-managers will benefit by reading it, too. The reason I'm starting with the managers is great customer experiences start at the top. If management supports customer experience initiatives and supports its people in customer interactions, it shows. If management is customer-friendly, the employees will more likely be customer-friendly. If your processes are customer-centric, the employee can be more customer-centric.

Many of us have had the experience of dealing with a nasty or uncaring employee at a company, store or restaurant only to find the manager or supervisor is just as nasty and uncaring. In business, the apple doesn't fall too far from the tree.

Whose Responsibility is the Customer Environment?

The manager has much to do with the environment in her department. She sets the tone; she creates the attitude employees have towards the customer, both external and internal; she models behavior that employees watch and mimic. If the manager is a team player and fosters a team environment, the employees know that they are expected to be team players, too.

This doesn't mean the employees don't have a huge role in creating and maintaining the environment. Employees need to have each other's backs. They must support each other and avoid sniping and gossiping. If a co-worker is doing good work, pat him on the back. If he does something exceptional, make sure everybody else knows. This shows you appreciate the effort.

Managers should be happy when it sometimes seems like the department or the team could operate on its own, without the manager. The more decisions team members can make on their own to benefit both the customer and the company without asking the boss, the better. It's not a question of ego; it's a question of whether the department is working together to serve the customer.

What Gets in the Way?

I showed a rough copy of this book to a few customer experience professionals (as well as some people who manned the lines in inbound call centers). I received pushback in a number of different areas, all of which have to do with internal and management issues:

> *People don't have the tools and authority to do many of the things you say we should do. If it comes down to getting my boss upset because I took authority and made a decision, I'm going to pass on taking initiative on the customer's behalf.*

When we count down to Chapter 3, I point out there are two types of rules – rules that cannot be broken under any circumstance and rules that can be bent for the sake of the customer. If I know that taking the initiative to make a decision regarding a customer problem could get me in serious trouble if it turns out to be wrong, I'm going to avoid making decisions. In many companies I've worked with, this problem frustrates customer-facing employees most – no authority. You can't have consistent "first call resolution" if your people are afraid to make decisions. Nobody wants to lose his job on the chance the supervisor doesn't agree with what he did.

I've worked with companies that have compliance requirements, sensitive issues, and major consequences if the employee makes the wrong decision. I understand companies need to protect themselves and in many cases, their customers. There are rules that they must follow and things they cannot do. This is a given.

In working with a major healthcare system, I was told often that healthcare professionals couldn't do certain things for patients or their families. When I asked why, I often received the same answer, "HIPAA." HIPAA stands for the Health Insurance Portability and Accountability Act, which protects patient privacy. Violating HIPAA is a major problem. All patient information, from major diagnoses to the smallest detail, needs to be guarded and protected.

For instance, an employee said she heard a colleague refer to a patient as "The *kidney* in room 451."

"The kidney? Why would she do that?" I asked.

"Because of HIPAA. We can't say the patient's name in a public setting, like the hallway. So she referred to him by his problem," she answered.

"But ... the *kidney*? Really? Can't she say, 'The patient in room 451,' or 'the gentleman' or 'the patient with the kidney condition in room 451?'"

Another class participant piped in and said, "A lot of people hide behind HIPAA, especially when they don't want to do something. Hiding behind HIPAA excuses a lot of sins."

Management can deal with these issues by being very clear about what authority and tools employees have and don't have in dealing with customer issues. Regulatory issues like HIPAA require more rules, other situations don't. It's not all or nothing.

According to *Giving Customer Voice More Volume*, a study from the CMO Council and Sabermetrix, only 29% of employees say they have a high ability to handle and resolve customer problems or complaints. This percentage virtually guarantees escalations, extended calls, and customer frustration.

> *I'd love to help my people learn all of this and to teach their supervisors how to coach them in the skills. But I have no budget for training. Sadly, the only real training they get is from their peers, which means that, in many cases, bad habits are being passed to new employees.*

I'm sure the skills and processes I talk about in this book will help you and your employees treat customers better and create great experiences. But a book can't change a culture, especially when the company doesn't provide for consistent reinforcement of skills. Yet I know too well the straitjacket leaders find themselves wearing when the company won't provide money (and time) for training, and I sympathize. Most of your people will not (or cannot) seek training outside of the company. Relatively few companies invest enough in their employees' growth and skills. Yet, there are those that do.

The companies in *Training Magazine's* 2011 Top 125 are committed to investing in their employees' growth. The magazine pointed out that the 125 companies "collectively dedicated an average 6.7% of their payroll to the training budget – and they have the business results to show for it." If you think that's too high for your organization, the magazine notes that its number one company, Farmer's Insurance, "only" spends 3.15% of payroll on training. Yours can spend less than that, and in many cases, still make a difference.

Reality says your company may not provide your people with the training they need, but reality also says that the customer experience skills in the following pages need to be taught, learned, practiced and reinforced. If it cannot be done in a formal setting, then it needs to be done informally. This is where the manager must take the initiative, even if it is something as small as borrowing a CD on coaching from the public library and learning how to coach.

Also, there needs to be agreement on whose responsibility it is for improving employee knowledge. Employees are asking, "To what extent am I expected to become a better, more efficient, learned employee 'on my own time' – which also translates to 'at my expense'?

Yes, I know that when something is important to me, I want to do it, but am I expected to teach myself at night and on weekends?"

Those are important questions. Whatever is in the budget – large or small – managers and employees need to work together to make sure skills are enhanced.

> *The advice you give is great. I'd love to use the words and communications processes you talk about. But I can only use the words and scripts they tell me to use – and I mean "word for word." The customer knows I'm using a script and of course, I know I'm using a script. And then [the company] tells me I'm not connecting with the customer.*

In Countdown Chapters 7, 6, 5, 4, 3 …well, in just about the entire book, I teach readers the words and ways to use those words to diffuse bad customer situations, make the customer feel like she is the most important person in the world, explain simple and difficult information, ask the right questions, say "no" without making the customer go ballistic, and more. These skills and words are essential in creating better customer experiences when customers interact with your people. But to use these skills, they must be able to be flexible to use the right words in the right situations. The less they rely on scripts, the more the customer will feel she is talking to a caring, customer-centric human being.

I understand the need for scripts. Customer-facing employees need to know what they can and cannot say, especially in highly regulated industries. If there are certain scripted responses needed in certain situations, by all means, require the scripts. But we've all called companies where the discussions over a problem had no legal ramifications and a script was used anyway. We could tell the CSR wasn't using her own words but was using a script instead.

A well-written script should cover most situations that come up in a meeting or phone call with a customer. Good scripts allow for a consistent message. But except in legal or regulatory situations, they should be guidelines, not word for word scripts.

Years ago, I was teaching business writing at a major airline. The airline named a new CEO and one of the first customer service moves he made was to prohibit "form letters," those "fill in the blank" documents that customers always knew were written the same way no matter who the customer was and what happened. Form letters were the scripts of their day. Within days, the customer service VP called me and set a date for me to teach her people how to write letters to customers.

The group of 55 people came to the class wary and frightened. During introductions, the first presenter approached the topic.

"We don't know what we're going to do! Do you know how many letters we send each day? What are we going to do without our form letters?"

I explained that while they would no longer write "form" letters, they would soon be writing "formula" letters. After writing dozens or even hundreds of individual letters, each representative would find a "formula" they would use for communicating with customers. But because they wouldn't be using a pre-written, scripted, form letter, each letter would be slightly- to very different depending on the customer and the situation. The letters would take little time to write and still be personalized. The same thing can happen with scripts.

I was amused recently when a call center director told me he needed training to stop people from relying *too much* on scripts. I asked if he'd ever criticized his people for saying the wrong thing. When he said yes, I told him that employees will do what's safest for their jobs. To paraphrase what I said in the answer about employee authority, management must have clear examples of when and why scripts are needed and when they're not, as well as how to use them.

Again, employees are not going to risk being fired or penalized by using their own words when they've been told not to. But if customers feel that the person on the other end of the line is an automated robot, they may fire your company.

> *This is very nice, but my people don't touch the customer. We work internally.*

As I'm sitting here typing away on my laptop, I'm not thinking about all the internal parts of the computer. I'm not thinking about the motherboard, the processor, the hard drive, the word processing software or anything else. All I know is the computer is working and I'm able to write my book. But that doesn't mean all of those things and more don't have everything to do with my success in completing the manuscript.

The people who put this laptop together for Dell have never spoken to me. They've never solved a problem I had, they've never seen my face, nor I theirs. The people in shipping may not have even noticed my name on the address label. And surely, they weren't thinking as they put the computer in the box, "Steve is going to *love* this!"

Yet each one of these people, wherever in the world they are located, has had a major effect on my using this machine. They did not write one word of the manuscript, but as you hold this book in your hands, you can give these people some credit for making it a reality.

The same thing goes for when things go wrong. Somebody, something, somewhere created the part or the system that went down on that particular morning, right in the middle of your needing it to work. And when customer service does or doesn't fix the issue as correctly or as quickly as we like, we blame the CSR.

Consider this situation:

The customer calls, saying she was double-billed for her monthly service. The customer service rep notices what the customer noticed, apologizes and says she will take care of it. The customer hangs up, the rep sends a message to billing, and billing is supposed to remove the second amount. But billing doesn't.

The customer calls again. The customer service rep assures her that she will take care of it and apologizes *again*. Again, the system doesn't allow the rep to remove the charge, so she sends it to billing and again the problem falls through the cracks. This time the customer calls back and the customer service rep connects her directly to billing, where somebody promises to "fix the problem." The amount is removed and everything is fine.

The next month, the same customer gets her bill and she is double-billed for the next month's charge. She calls and starts the process all over again. A few days after the final interaction, during which the customer screams and yells, she receives an email asking for feedback. As you might expect, she is none too happy and her ratings and statements reflect that. The higher ups send a note to customer service asking why they received such a bad review. But customer service wasn't responsible for that issue; billing was. So why was customer service blamed?

Recently, I've had the pleasure of meeting and getting to know Bill Price, the co-author (with David Jaffe) of *The Best Service is No Service: How to Liberate Your Customers from Customer Service, Keep Them Happy & Control Costs*. One of the book's major tenets is "own the actions across the company." As Bill and David say, "It is time to stop blaming the customer service department, which in the vast majority of cases, is the messenger and not the cause of customer contacts."

The book points out that the customer service manager and the CSRs are blamed for long queues, backlogs in responding to customer email, processing claims or any number of other issues. Bill says, "If you look a little deeper at why the customer contacts are occurring and what the staff needs to do to handle these contacts, then accountability of ownership appears less clear." Overall, customer service doesn't generate the calls (Price and Jaffe put the number at no more than 20%); the departments that are causing the problems or issues are causing people to call. Price says the costs and blame for customer dissatisfaction should be spread to the areas that cause the problems and not segregated to customer care. I agree.

Every employee at a company, as well as sub-contractors, free-lancers, and temps, has an effect on the customer's happiness. The customer doesn't care if your contractors didn't do their jobs. The customer doesn't care if it was the woman in shipping who put on the wrong label. The customer doesn't blame the shipping employee. The customer blames the company.

Everybody touches the customer. This needs to be a clear message from the top to all departments and areas, whether they directly deal with the customer or not.

> *These ideas are all well and good, but I can't find good people.*

Oh yeah you can. How come Southwest Airlines has no trouble finding good people? How come Land's End has no trouble finding good people? And if you're talking about finding people for the lower-paying jobs, how come Publix and Wegman's supermarkets don't have trouble finding good people?

But it's not just having good people that leads to great customer experiences. It's having a good customer culture. Take the people who work for Southwest, Land's End, Publix and Wegman's and put them in another company in the same sector and odds are they will not perform as well. Yes, you have to find good people to begin with, but you also need to nurture them, value them, teach them, and create a culture where employees understand their own importance to the success of the company and their importance to the customer experience. If you don't, you will find yourself saying, "I can't find good people."

On the way out of town during a business trip, I ordered a sandwich from an airport fast food location. The woman behind the counter didn't smile once, make a pleasant comment, or seem like she cared. She made me feel like I was bothering her. On the way back, I stopped at another fast food counter (yeah, I know – I eat too much fast food). This time, the woman behind the counter smiled, asked me where I was going and exchanged all sorts of pleasantries. I complimented her as I left, just as her supervisor was approaching. He thanked me for thanking her and visiting them. What was the difference between the two stores?

Surly people aren't always made surly by the job and happy

people aren't always made happy by the job. More often than not, they're hired that way.

I'll cover hiring good customer people at the end of this chapter in the "Manager Lift-Off" section.

Co-Workers are Also Customers

When I ask employees, "What gets in the way?" one of the top items on the list is "Co-workers don't follow through." Co-workers are also customers and it's as important to follow through for your fellow employees as it is to follow through for external customers.

I often ask people, "Do you think we sometimes treat our internal customers differently than we do our external customers?" Most people say "yes," probably because it's true. We tend to see our external customers as those who are of the utmost importance and the people we work with as secondary. There's also a tendency for people to see it as management's responsibility to create a working environment and a "team" atmosphere. Nothing could be further from the truth.

First, there is no reason to treat our internal customers poorly or anything less than exceptionally. Every person affects the customer experience. Second, everything these people do affects you. If they do a great job, you have a better day. If they go the extra mile for you, your life is easier. If they show up every day, you don't have to pick up their slack. Working every day in an unhappy department is like living every day in an unhappy family.

There's an old expression, "Familiarity breeds contempt." Never have I seen this with such regularity as in the workplace. I was observing a few employees at a company we were preparing to serve when the phone rang on one of the employees' desks. The employee picked up and said, "Good morning, welcome to [blah-blah] company. How may I help you?" I was impressed at the businesslike but friendly greeting he made to this customer.

A couple of minutes after he got off the phone with the customer, the phone rang again, but this time with a different ring. He picked up the phone and said in a tone that indicated he was being bothered, "Yeah?"

After that call was done (in a totally different way than the first call), I walked over to his desk. I told him what I had observed and asked, "Why was the second call so different from the first call?"

"The first call was a customer. The second call was Darrell from contracts," he answered with a half-smile.

"So the second call was internal and the first call was external, am I correct?"

"Yeah. I've *got* to talk to my customers in a nice way. Darrell, on the other hand, annoys me. He calls me with questions *all* the time."

I wasn't astonished by this answer, but I wish I was because that would mean it was out of the ordinary, but it isn't. Differentiating external customers and internal customers happens like this in just about every company. Still, I continued the conversation.

"What do you think would happen if you treated your external customer the way you treated Darrell?" I asked.

"That's a ridiculous question. I would never treat my customers that way. They may never buy from us again." Then, a look came on his face that said he knew where I was going with this. He said, "I can't let the customer know I'm annoyed because there are consequences. They could walk away and never do business with us again. Also, they could ask to speak to my supervisor, and if you think I was annoyed at Darrell, you should see how my boss feels about me when a call is escalated.

"However, I know Darrell. I've even gone to lunch with him once or twice. He's okay with the attitude. I mean, he's not going to leave his job because I didn't treat him well."

I made a point of focusing on internal customers in the class the next day.

We spend almost 50% of our waking hours doing something

having to do with our jobs. We see the people we work with just about as often as we see our families. One would hope your relationship with your family members is filled with respect, care, and mutual support. Your work family deserves the same.

IT BEGINS WITH YOU

Most issues with customers are *people* issues. People deal with each other, work with each other, cooperate with each other, or don't cooperate with each other. People make rules that are written down and rules they assume everybody understands.

Almost every issue I've touched in this chapter has to do with communication and stepping outside ourselves to see the world through the customer's eyes, both external and internal customers. Communication is a *people* issue. Management is a *people* issue.

The skills in this book will help you and if you're a manager, your people deal with customer issues and create an experience customers will remember for a long time. But customer experience is more than being nice. People need to have the ability, the flexibility, and the authority to do the things they need to do.

If you're not a manager, this doesn't get you off the hook. Blaming the manager or the system for your inability to create great experiences is easy, but it's not the whole story. In the end, we may or may not have the authority to do certain things or overcome issues. But we do have the ability to overcome attitude issues. We can blame our attitudes on our bosses, but that doesn't change anything. We can let the things people say to us bother us; that just gives them the power.

An old song says, "Let there be peace on earth and let it begin with me." This statement applies greatly to what we do when working with customers.

It begins with you. It *always* begins with you. You may not be able to fix an internal issue or process, but if given the authority and the knowledge, you can figure out how to explain the issue or work around it. You can figure out what you can do for the customer so the internal issue isn't that big of an issue. You can tell the person who is responsible for the internal issue that it is standing in the way of your being the best customer advocate you can be.

It begins with you. It *always* begins with you. You can decide that the customer is being a royal pain and you don't want to help her. But that won't fix the problem, and eventually, the problem will come back and bite you, either from that customer or from another.

It's not rocket service.

Rocket Review

- The department- and company environment have a huge effect on how employees treat customers and the level of customer happiness.

- Employees have as huge a role in establishing a customer-centric environment as their managers do.

- People need the tools and authority to take care of customer issues. Manager involvement in customer problems should be the exception, not the rule.

- Even a small amount of training will help your employees serve customers better. Large training budgets are nice to have, but small (or no) training budgets are no excuse for not doing some kind of training.

- Employees will not risk being fired for taking authority where there is none or deviating from scripts even if they think there's a better way.

- Co-workers are customers. They are as important as external customers.

Manager Lift-Off

You can hire people and try to teach them to be good customer people or you can hire good customer people and teach them the skills they need to be outstanding. An old customer service statistic says that 68% of customers stop doing business with a company because of the way they were treated, while only 14% stopped because of the product. The single most important thing you can do to assure positive customer interactions is to hire the right people before unleashing them on your customers.

A Chief Customer Officer at a client asked me my thoughts on hiring good customer people – not necessarily good customer service representatives – but people who are good with customers. Instead of answering him immediately, I asked him a few questions.

I asked him to give me an example of a question he asks potential hires.

He said he always asks them to give an example of how they handled a tough situation, which is a very good question. If an employee can't handle a tough situation properly, you're going to have a lot of angry customers. Then I asked him "What percentage of interactions are difficult?" He answered that bad calls happen a lot less often than it seems, yet we always remember the bad calls. He finally admitted the number was probably just under 10%. Yet the first question he came up with was that one.

I then told him that he should instead say, "Tell me about a situation where you were able to make a customer happy" and then sit back, watch and listen. Do her eyes brighten when she talks about the customer and what happened? Does she smile a lot during the story? How enthusiastic is she about the result?

I advised him that after the candidate finishes that answer, he should ask two questions: "Why do you think that made the customer happy?" and "Why are you so happy about making the customer happy?" He should be able to know whether to continue the discussion after that first question and the follow-up questions. If her eyes didn't light up, if she didn't smile during the best parts of the story, and if there was no enthusiasm, this person is not going to do well when the going gets tough. (By the way, if a candidate has never worked in a customer-facing job before, ask him if he has any pets. Then ask him to tell you about the pet. Look for the same things; it'll tell you a lot about his character. You don't want somebody working for you who can't say enthusiastic, nice things about his dog.)

After that, I might follow-up with the question about difficult customers.

Here are some more thoughts on what to look for when hiring good customer people:

Besides enthusiasm in the voice, smiles on the face, and joy in the eyes, look at how confident they are. (You've got to be confident to deal with customers all day, every day.)

Do they speak clearly? How is their voice tone? Make sure you hear empathy in their voice when they're talking about a sad or difficult situation. It never fails to amaze me when I find people mumbling, showing no empathy, and being monotone when talking to customers. Never mind whether they can learn to serve customers better. How did they get hired for a *call center* or any customer-facing position in the first place?

How do they get along with others? Make sure you station a friendly person in the room where the candidate sits before the interview. Have the friendly person start a conversation with the candidate. If the candidate doesn't respond to the conversation, there may be a problem. Customer people need to engage customers when the customer starts a conversation.

I hate to say it, but you may want to make the candidate wait awhile for the interview. Ask your friendly person to watch how patient or impatient the candidate is.

A few years ago, I heard a story about a supermarket chain in Texas that would schedule several interviews for management training positions at the same time and put all the candidates in the same room prior to the interviews. They would then watch the candidates through a one-way mirror as they waited. The candidates who talked to others or made an effort to be friendly earned points, while the candidates whose noses stayed buried in a book or magazine and those who sat alone or made no contact with the others lost points. The theory is if you have a propensity to interact with and like people, even in a tense situation like a job interview, you will be a better manager. (Why companies hire managers without people skills is a question for another book.)

When you're giving the candidate information about the job, is she listening? Or does she look like she can't wait to jump in with another comment? On the same hand, does she ask questions and show interest?

Ask the candidate how your product or service touches your customer on a human level. For instance, if you're hiring for a bank, ask how the bank touches customers' lives. Probe for emotions. Make sure they understand the impact your organization has on its customers. (If you make a product that is less well known to the public, tell the candidate a little about the product and then ask the same question.)

After the interview, send the candidate an email with a few additional questions. Look at the reply, especially if this person will be corresponding with customers. Is it grammatically correct? How's the spelling? Are the questions answered in a conversational style or are the answers abrupt? Does the candidate open with a salutation and close with his or her name? Or are those things just left out? Do you get the warm fuzzies?

This brings me to some more radical, but effective things you might do. If you're hiring the person to talk to customers on a chat line, do the interview on a chat. See how she writes and expresses herself in that format. The same goes for those who work with customers on the phone. You may want to do an in-person interview later, but this is a good start for those jobs.

If the work environment will be noisy while she talks to customers, interview her in a noisy environment. See how it affects her. If she is easily distracted from the conversation, she'll be easily distracted from the customer.

Ask her to do something she more than likely can't (like get a recommendation from her 5th grade teacher). Watch how she reacts. It could come in handy later when she has to explain bad news to a customer.

You may be asking, "Aren't you going to tell me to ask how they would handle certain tough situations or how they should treat customers?"

No. Those things, as well as how to greet customers, ask

questions, explain information, and go the extra mile are skills employees will learn later, through training – classroom, peer-to-peer, online, or otherwise. People who deal with customers all day need to be comfortable and enthusiastic about working with people. The idea of making someone's day better should excite them. Not having the ability to do what the customer needs or wants should disappoint them. Think of all the times you heard "There's nothing we can do" and felt the representative couldn't care less.

You can hire people and try to teach them to be good customer people or you can hire good customer people and teach them the skills they need to be outstanding. It will make all the difference.

COUNTDOWN:

It's Not About You

I had just finished speaking at a conference when a member of the audience walked up to me and handed me a pay stub from her recent paycheck. I wasn't quite sure why this woman wanted me to see her pay stub, unless it was to show me that she made more money than I did.

I looked at her quizzically and before I could say anything, she said, "Look what it says on the bottom of the pay stub." I glanced down and there it was: a revelation that told me this company gets it.

"This paycheck is brought to you by your customers."

My eyes grew wide and so did my smile. This company reminded its people every other week just who was responsible for the company's success and that without that success, there would be no company. And there would be no job.

They could have communicated this by putting a huge poster on the wall that says, "We love our customers," but that wouldn't have made the impact that seeing this statement associated with the employee's pay has made – and continues to make – with each payday. In other words, the food you put on your table, the car you just bought, the college education you're paying for, the ability to pay the mortgage, the vacation in the Bahamas and that new videogame system are all brought to you by your customers. What nice people they are to give you this money!

Now, we know you worked very hard and you're very good at what you do, but in the end, if the customer doesn't pay the bills, there's no work for you to do.

Customers are your best friends. They make sure your salary is paid. Or, if you're in your own business, they make sure you make a profit and remain in business. That's why it's never about you.

Think about how you treat your best friends. If they've been good friends for a long time, you're clearly doing something right. You're probably putting their needs before yours, giving them the benefit of the doubt, and sharing the responsibilities for whatever you decide to do together. In other words, when you're best friends, you make it about them and they make it about you. Think about a time when you got into a fight with your best friend. Odds are that something happened where you made it about you (or vice versa).

CAN A CUSTOMER BE UNREASONABLE?

Of course, a customer can be unreasonable! But that doesn't matter. It doesn't matter if he was being unreasonable, being selfish, or having a tantrum on the roof of your building. It doesn't matter if he screams at you on the phone.

It's not about you. It's about him. This is the first and most overriding rule of good customer relationships: *It's not about you.*

One of the sad facts of business most people choose to ignore (or never learned) is that it is never about *you*. Interactions with customers are never about what *you* want, what *you* need, what *you* care about, or anything else having to do with *you*. If you want to matter to your customers, nothing about *you* should matter. This is especially true when customers are upset.

If your customer is angry, deal with it. *It's not about you.*

If your customer wants you to go the extra mile, do it. *It's not about you.*

If your customer wants you to do something faster, do what you can to get it done more quickly. *It's not about you.*

If your customer has had a bad day and takes it out on you, that's too bad. *It's not about you.*

If your customer has a certain way of doing things that is effective, try to work within that system. *It's not about you.*

If your customer is a horse's you-know-what, even then, *it's not about you.* (This doesn't include abusive customers. That's a subject for when we count down to Chapter 6.)

Is the Customer Always Right?

A number of years ago, I interviewed a major retail executive. He proudly took me to a large stone that stood at the entrance of the store. Engraved on the stone was the following:

Rule # 1: **The customer is always right.**

Rule # 2: **If the customer is ever wrong, re-read rule #1.**

Statements like this one have plagued employees and companies forever. This simplistic sentiment is repeated over and over like a mantra in training, marketing, and the media. But there's a problem: it's not true. Take any group of employees and tell them "the customer is always right," and somebody will say, "But what if the customer really is wrong? Sometimes, they are." The simple statement the executive showed me is not so simple. But as I said, *it's not rocket service.* Here's a simpler statement:

Rule #1: **The customer is not always right.**

Rule #2: ***But* the customer is always the most important person in the conversation.**

It's worth repeating.

The customer is not always right, but the customer is always the most important person in the conversation.

Does that make you feel better? Anybody who preaches that the customer is always right is setting the employee up for failure. One of these days, sooner rather than later, a customer is going to be wrong, really wrong, and the employees won't know what to do. It is better to say the customer is not always right, but the customer is always the most important person in the conversation. Whether the customer is right or wrong (or somewhere in between), your job is to try to resolve the issue to the customer's satisfaction. You can give her the refund or find a more creative way to satisfy her.

In a recent customer service training class, one of the participants told of receiving a call from a customer who asked her many, many questions. The customer kept her on the phone for what seemed to be an eternity. After the service rep explained everything, she asked the customer if he was clear on the information. The customer replied, "Yeah, thanks. That's exactly what it says right here on your website."

The service rep told me she was beside herself. She said, "Can you believe that man was looking right at the website while he was talking to me and was reading everything I was telling him? What a waste of my time!"

I asked, "How did you respond?"

"I told him, 'You really could have just looked at the website and not called me. All I did was tell you everything you were already seeing on the site.' He replied, 'Well, I just wanted to make sure all of the information was correct.'"

I could see she was getting agitated all over again as she told the story.

"And now you're upset that you spent all of this time with this customer when you could have been doing something else," I said.

"Yes, I was so annoyed. I mean, he can *read*, can't he?"

I replied, "But *it's not about you*. It's not about whether he could have gotten the same information just by looking at the website. It doesn't matter that he didn't need to call you. *He* thought he needed to call you, and that's why you're there."

The customer is the most important person in the conversation. *It's not about you.*

Let me tell you a story about my grandfather.

Grandpa Max owned a men's clothing store in a working-class neighborhood in Brooklyn, NY. My grandfather owned the store for more than 45 years and my father worked at his side for more than 25 years. It was a family business that served people and treated customers like family.

When I was 16, I spent the summer working in the store several days a week for my father and grandfather. Summers were very quiet in the store because most people had shopped for men's clothing by Father's Day. One afternoon, a man walked into the store with a pair of pants slung over his arm and said, "Max, I need to return these pants. They just don't fit right."

I took a look at the pants he was carrying and knew immediately that he had done more than just try them on. After my grandfather gently tried to talk the man out of returning the pants, he finally relented and took the pants back. But he never commented on their condition.

When the man left the store, I turned to my grandfather and said, "Grandpa, I'm sure he wore those pants."

He gave me a quick wave of the hand. I persisted.

"Grandpa, he definitely wore those pants. Why did you let him return them?"

Without even looking at me, he said, "Steven, the man lives in the neighborhood. His wife shops here and so does his mother. He goes to the big church across the street. And he frequents the many bars in the neighborhood. You know what happens when people are drinking a little bit? They talk. I don't want him sitting at the bar telling everybody about 'that S.O.B Max' who wouldn't let him return the pants. This is a neighborhood store."

Grandpa had a choice. He could have refused to take back the pants, saying in other words that the man was a liar. Had he not allowed the man to return the pants, he might have been right. But he would have had one angry customer with lots of friends who would listen. Instead, he kept his reputation and had happy customers who came back again and again.

Grandpa always made it about the customers who frequented his store. His store survived 45 years, including the Great Depression, war, good times and bad times. People spread the good news that Max and Arnold were fair guys and their store was a good place to shop.

They'll Make It About You

Forget anything that has to do with you. When you make it about customers, they'll make it about you. Treat them as the most important people in the conversation, and they'll have positive conversations about you. If you resolve their situation quickly, they'll immediately think of you when they want to recommend somebody. If you treat them as relationship partners, they will do the same. Get into the mindset that the first and most important thing is solving the customer's problem or responding to her request.

Still, I can hear you saying, "But if I always do what the customer wants me to do, I'll go out of business. There's a difference between being nice to the customer and giving away the store!"

I agree wholeheartedly. I would never want you to jeopardize your business to make the customer happy. I would never want you to "give away the store." All I'm saying is that if you treat the customer as the most important person in the conversation you will make the right choice on the best course of action. Maybe you'll give her the refund and maybe you won't. Perhaps you'll find another way to make her happy. Maybe she'll never be happy, but she will appreciate that you tried to help.

When you make it about customers, they'll make it about you.

It's not rocket service.

Rocket Review

- Employee paychecks are paid for by customer purchases and loyalty. They are the most important people in your business life.

- Always remember this one thing: *It's Not About You.*

- There are two rules of customer relationships: Rule #1: The customer is not always right; Rule #2: But the customer is always the most important person in the conversation.

- If you make it about them, they'll make it about you.

Manager Lift-Off

What are you communicating to your people about customers, both in actions and words? Are you telling them that it's all about what the company wants, what's easy for you or your department, or what's best for the bottom line? Or do you tell them that the customer is the most important person in the conversation? Are you giving your people the authority to make it about the customer, or do they have to go through you to bend the rules? Are they pressured to "stick to the script" or are they told (as they do at Nordstrom's), "Use good judgment in all that you do"?

Your words and actions will communicate who comes first in employee considerations. Employees will do what they feel you are paying them to do. If they get the impression that policies and procedures are more important than customer happiness, they will stick to the policies and procedures and forget about the customer. If you don't give them the authority to make decisions as a customer advocate, then you'll be inundated with escalations. When your people have the tools and techniques to serve the customer and the authority to make those decisions, you will not be called to help solve customer issues and you will have more time to do "manager stuff."

Employees pay more attention to what you do than what you say. Make sure your actions send the right messages about customer engagement.

COUNTDOWN:

Expectations Drive Everything

During the past 15 years or so, I have spent time in the offices of more than 150 different companies and organizations. The good thing about being a consultant is that I notice things in an office that the average employee doesn't because to him it's just part of the scenery. It's similar to when a new store opens in that strip mall down the street and you can't remember what store was there before the new one. It was just part of the scenery.

I notice these things because I'm looking with "fresh eyes." And one of the first things I notice are the messages management sends to the employees. One of the messages I often see is "exceed expectations." It might be a motivational poster or a mission statement. Sometimes, the company (or a particular manager) will post articles on the bulletin board in the break room with titles like the following:

- "How to Exceed Expectations"
- "Exceeding Customer Expectations Is More Than Just Providing Great Service"
- "Are You Exceeding Expectations?"
- "Exceed Expectations and You'll Have Happy Customers Forever"
- "Go the Extra Mile: Exceed Expectations"

Several companies have gone so far as to include "exceed expectations" in their goals, mission or values statements which they then put on a large plaque that hangs somewhere in the front of the office. The message is clear: this company cares about exceeding expectations. Meeting expectations is just not enough.

I totally agree with that sentiment and we'll address how to exceed expectations when we count down to Chapter 1. Yet after I see those plaques and articles on the walls and bulletin boards, I walk around the office, looking for the plaque that lists what the customer's expectations are.

And I never find it.

How can you exceed customer expectations if you don't know what they are? It's like shooting at a target without being able to see it.

EVERYTHING IN LIFE IS ABOUT EXPECTATIONS

Most companies and people have no idea what their customers expect from them. They *think* they know, but few people take the time to ask their customers to identify their expectations. This is scary because your success depends on knowing that information.

Whether your customers are internal or external, they have certain expectations. How they feel about you, your product and your company is based on how well you meet or exceed their expectations. A customer's expectations are the chief determining factor in customer happiness and loyalty.

Frankly, our expectations determine the way we feel about almost anything. *Everything* in life is about expectations. Every judgment you make and every opinion you have is based on your expectations. When I'm on my way to work in the morning and need to buy gas for my car, I decide whether the price of gas at a certain station is high or low based on what I expect it should be. If the price was $2.75 a gallon yesterday, I expect something similar today.

During the past few years, though, gas prices have been all over the map. One day, the price was $4.20 a gallon. Outrageous! So, imagine what your reaction would have been if, a couple of days later, you go to the gas station and find that the price had dropped to $3.25. You would be thrilled – thrilled that the price is $3.25 after it had been $4.20 just a few days before. What a great price! With that kind of price difference, you would run home to get your spouse's car and fill that tank, too!

A few months later, the price dropped significantly to about $1.75 a gallon. So, imagine what your reaction would be if a couple of days after that you go to the gas station and find that the price had gone up to $3.25. You would be so angry! The price was $3.25 after being $1.75 just a few days before. Outrageous!

Same price, different expectations.

My friend Ken Futch told me the following story to show me how I could be unhappy with a $10,000 raise.

Your boss calls you into his office and tells you to close the door. He tells you that you have been doing such a good job that he's going to give you a $10,000 raise. But, he tells you, you can't tell anybody.

You go back to your cubicle and you're bursting with excitement. You know somebody might overhear your conversation if you call your wife to tell her, and you promised your boss you wouldn't tell anybody. However, you can't stand it anymore and you go to your buddy, Bill, whom you can trust with anything. You pull him aside and whisper, "Bill, I'm not supposed to tell anybody, but the boss just gave me a $10,000 raise!' Bill looks at you and says, '$10,000? That's funny. The rest of us got $20,000."

When you expect no raise at all, $10,000 sounds phenomenal. When you discover that everybody but you is getting $20,000, you feel cheated because your raise is only $10,000. Expectations determine your reactions to everything.

HIGH EXPECTATIONS = HIGH REWARDS

When my daughter was 16, I had a discussion with her about people's expectations. In a typical teenage way, she turned to me and said, "Well Dad, if people are going to judge you based on their expectations, shouldn't you try to keep people's expectations low? If they don't expect too much, it's easy to fulfill their expectations. They won't be disappointed." I told her that it was an interesting thought but that in the end it doesn't make a person successful. Higher expectations bring higher rewards if you meet or exceed them. Lower expectations bring lower rewards.

When an Olympic diver receives a rating from the judges, it is multiplied by the degree of difficulty. A rating of 8 on a dive with a degree of difficulty of 3.5 gets a higher score than a rating of 10 with a degree of difficulty of 2.0. High or low expectations work the same way.

You expect certain behaviors, actions, and results from different individuals, different companies, and different stores. When I walk into a Lexus dealer, or a very high-end steakhouse, I have certain expectations – very high expectations. The price they charge may have something to do with the high expectations, but those expectations also come from reputation, word of mouth, and marketing. I wouldn't expect the people at a Lexus dealer to treat me how I would be treated at a local used car lot. But here's the question: *should* the dealer at the local used car lot treat you the same way as the Lexus dealer?

At a seminar for a mid-priced car company, I made the above point about what I would expect at a Lexus dealership. The topic came up when one of the managers mentioned that he had bought a Lexus before working for this particular company. He mentioned that Lexus had luxury down pat. He listed the things they did:

- There were no "vultures" standing outside the dealership waiting to pounce on unsuspecting customers. In fact, the dealership encouraged potential buyers to make appointments so that someone would be ready to assist them personally upon their arrival.

- When he walked into the dealership, a concierge offered him a drink. When he asked for a Diet Coke, the concierge brought the drink in a glass with ice. She then introduced him to a salesperson, who walked him into an office. The salesperson was well dressed and not pushy at all.

- Before looking at cars, the salesperson took some time to get to know him – his likes, dislikes, his experiences with other dealers, and of course, his family. The office looked like an executive's office.

- When showing him the car, the salesperson opened the door to the vehicle, made sure the buyer was comfortable in the car, and took time, time, and more time to allow the buyer to become one with the automobile. At the end of this experience, my seminar participant said he felt as if this car had been part of his life forever.

When he shared his story, I asked about his customer service experiences at the dealership since he bought the car. His answer was effusive, explaining that they took the same time and attention when he came in for check ups, repairs, and inspections. He told how the salesperson called him on his birthday, sent flowers to his wife on Mother's Day, and in general, created an ongoing relationship. I asked if they met his expectations. He said, "I expected a lot, but not that much."

I asked the car company group, "So what do you think of that?" After several seminar attendees smiled and looked at each other, a brave attendee raised her hand and said, "Well, they're Lexus. That's what they do. We're not Lexus."

"So what did the Lexus people do that we can't do? Can we give one on-one attention to the customer? Can our salespeople look nice? Can we look at the customer as a person and not as the sum total of his purchases? Can we personally follow up on a regular basis and not just with a free oil change coupon? How much do these things cost?" I asked.

"But that's not what they expect from us. They expect a lot more from Lexus," she answered. Somebody else in the room then piped in, "That doesn't mean we can't be as good as Lexus. There's nothing the people at Lexus can do that we're not capable of doing."

I couldn't have said it any better myself. They later came up with a list of ways to offer this kind of service to their customers.

Employees in many companies have an attitude that assumes their customer's expectations are based on the price they pay or the level of product they sell. In most cases, they're right. But there really shouldn't be anything physically holding them back from treating customers in the "Lexus" way, no matter what product or service they are offering or what the customer's expectations are.

"Crazy" Attitudes

Years ago, there was an electronics chain in New York called Crazy Eddie. Its commercials featured this crazy guy screaming at the top of his lungs about the store's phenomenal prices. The tag line was "Crazy Eddie! His prices are insane!"

Crazy Eddie promised that if you found the same product at another store for less money he would match it or come in lower. They made sure they had the cheapest prices in town ... and they treated you that way.

The floor sales staff seemed to have this attitude that said, "You're too cheap to spend any more money than you can spend here, so we're going to treat you like the cheap person you are." Shoppers were treated as if they were ignorant about the products and not worth the staff's time. And God forbid you showed a coupon with a lower price than theirs. They would accept it – begrudgingly.

Consumers expected that Crazy Eddie's people would treat them poorly, but they also expected low, low prices. So they prepared themselves for bad service, knowing that at least they were getting a good price. Several years after Crazy Eddie and other low-price electronics stores who treated customers the same way established their market, newer, low-cost chains like Best Buy and hhgregg began to take over.

Both companies made a commitment to provide knowledgeable employees and services that said, "We want you as a customer." While performance at individual stores may vary, overall, both Best Buy and hhgregg have received high ratings from organizations such as JD Power and Associates and *Fortune* magazine. In JD Power's

2010 survey of customers at home appliance retailers, both chains received a 4 out of 5 rating on overall satisfaction, while hhgregg received a perfect score on "Sales, staff and service."

Best Buy introduced such customer-friendly policies as allowing shoppers to order online and pick up the item at the nearest store. They have positioned themselves as the place to go for tech advice, addressing something many customers feel insecure about. On any matter, store staffers take a hands-on approach to hunt down answers to customer questions, including finding a product that its stores don't carry. In an article in the *Columbus (OH) Dispatch*, an industry analyst went into a Best Buy store and asked an employee about a tripod for an iPhone. The incognito analyst was impressed when the employee went online in the store and found a $14 version on eBay.

"Best Buy didn't make a dollar," the analyst, Stephen Baker of NPD Group, said. "But he did something that you can't find anywhere else."

Both chains are succeeding because they not only have low prices but they also exceed customers' low expectations by treating them better. Once the expectations changed, places like Crazy Eddie lost their customer base.

SENDING THE MESSAGE

The owner of a cell phone store in Michigan hired me to teach his people how to sell more phones. The store was located in a downtown business district and his clientele was 80% businesspeople. The store was well positioned to service these customers and from the outside had the appearance of a store that served the corporate market.

Now, we've all seen wireless telephone stores and kiosks populated by part-time, teenage employees who look and act as if they'd rather be hanging with their friends than helping customers. When you leave these kiosks, you feel as though you should have gone to a different store. That was not the case with this store.

When I walked into the store, I was met by a well-dressed young woman who asked how she could help me. While she went to get the storeowner, I watched the other employees work with customers. First, each employee was well dressed. The young men wore shirts, ties and slacks. The young women wore blouses and skirts or dress slacks or a pants/jacket combination. None of the employees looked to be a day over 23, yet none of them displayed excessive piercings on their face or ears or had visible tattoos. And when they spoke to the customers, they were mature, polite and handled themselves professionally. They clearly understood their customer's expectations.

I was quite impressed and mentioned so to the storeowner. I asked, "How do you do it? Where did you find such great young people?" He replied that he was very picky when it came to hiring, even though he didn't pay any more than the other dealers in town. He then said, "Most importantly, they know what I expect of them. I'm very clear on my expectations. Even though most of them are teenagers, I told them there was no reason they couldn't behave as adults or look professional. My store is in a business area. We sell to businesspeople. I expect my people to work, behave, and look like businesspeople."

Expectations not only dictate what customers expect of us but also what we expect of ourselves. Is there any reason why someone who works for a mid-priced car dealer can't treat customers like a Lexus employee would? Is there any reason you can't expect a teenager working a part-time job to behave as a professional? Should the price you pay dictate what you should expect from the store or company with whom you do business? I don't think so.

It's not rocket service.

WHAT DO YOUR CUSTOMERS EXPECT?

I ask this question in my classes all the time. I break the class into groups and ask them to make a list of their customers' expectations. They dive into this exercise with great abandon, reaching into the database of experiences that resides in their brains. They remember the times the customer was upset and the days the customer was so happy she kissed them! They're ready to tell me what they know about their customers, the customer's expectations, and how well they're meeting those expectations. Here are a few that come up almost all the time:

- Do what you say you're going to do.
- Do what they want you to do.
- Be polite.
- Care.
- Be prompt and on time.
- Do it quickly.
- Show empathy.
- Treat me as a person, not an account number.
- Bend the rules for me.
- Don't make me repeat myself.
- Know what you are talking about.
- Don't transfer me.

Depending on the business or organization, there can be many more. After they reveal their lists, I ask them, "Are these expectations high? Are they unreasonable?" The answer is almost always no, and they're absolutely correct.

Expectations aren't right or wrong, good or bad. They are not high or low. They just *are*. And here's the bad news: If you do all of the things they expect, you're nothing special because they *expect* you to do those things.

You're nothing special. You've met their expectations, which is what they expected you to do. They're not going to pat you on the back. It's like when somebody complains, "Hey, I do my job but you don't appreciate me." I know you do your job. I expect you to do your job. I'm not going to reward you for meeting my expectations.

Your customers aren't going to reward you either. Meeting

expectations is not enough. Anybody can do that. But can you exceed your customers' expectations? That's where the difference between you and your competition resides.

WHERE DO EXPECTATIONS COME FROM?

Expectations don't just appear out of thin air. They not only come from our experiences but also from the messages we receive from the company and others. These messages fall into four categories: advertising, promises, branding and word of mouth.

Advertising
A few years ago, airlines began adding something to their flights that really got me excited: little TV screens on the back of the seats so you could watch television programs, movies and other entertainment during your flight. I fly a lot, so I was thrilled that I could fly from Minneapolis to Atlanta and watch the ballgame. How great is that?

The first summer after these TV screens became available the airlines advertised the dickens out of it. I'm a huge baseball fan, and in Atlanta, the Braves are the team to watch and I watch them just about every night. Three or four times during the game, I saw commercials about TV screens on flights. Sure enough, the first time I flew that summer, I watched TV during my flight.

Then the airline industry ran into financial difficulties and moved many of the "large airplane" flights to regional carriers, which cost less to run. Even the Atlanta-Newark route, which always featured large planes, featured regional carriers. The regional carriers have no movies and no TV.

So, after seeing the commercials all summer and then actually experiencing the TVs on a couple of flights, I was very disappointed when I stopped seeing them on the flights I took. I would find my seat and utter under my breath, "Well, no TVs on this flight. It's a two-hour flight. It's the least they can do."

Does an airline have a responsibility to provide me with TV on my flights? Should that be an expected part of airline service? Probably not, but when they *told* me they would have TV screens on their planes, they set my expectations. If they had never told me they had TVs on the planes, I wouldn't have looked for them.

We first create expectations through the company's advertising. Advertising causes people to buy. It defines the brand, which includes expectations. Lexus's brand: high expectations. Crazy Eddie: low expectations. If your advertising tells me that you have the best product, I have a right to expect that you have the best.

Branding
A brand defines who you are, how you do things, and what differentiates you from your competition. It creates a promise. By doing so, it establishes expectations. Just the mention of a particular brand creates characteristics and thereby expectations in customers minds.

The Lexus story earlier told of what Lexus does to create a great customer experience. But even if you've never been in a Lexus dealership or purchased a Lexus, you have an expectation of that company and its products. When a brand is strong, a huge majority of people will state the same expectation when the brand name is mentioned.

What are your expectations of the following brands?

- Chevrolet
- Tiffany
- Apple
- Starbucks
- Walmart
- Disney

Disney refers to its theme parks as "the happiest place on earth." Hearing that, what are your expectations of the experiences you will have there?

Have you ever met anyone who went to a Disney park and had a lousy time? People have a great time at Disney and therefore others have high expectations of their own Disney experience. Even though customers come with high expectations, Disney seems to meet and exceed them consistently.

I once heard a speaker at a conference say, "No matter who you compete against, you're competing against the world and every experience your customer has ever had with any business. You're not competing against your competition, you're competing against Disney."

Here's an interesting exercise. Next time you're watching TV or reading a magazine, make a list of the first 10 brands that are mentioned or whose advertisements you see. Then, write down the first customer expectation you would have of that brand. After you've done so, take the list and show it to four other people. Ask them to write down their customer expectations. My feeling is the five of you will have said similar things.

Your brand infers a promise. Be careful what you promise; promises create expectations. People make their plans based on expectations.

Promises
My friend Eileen had a problem with another airline. She also travels quite a bit and had accrued quite a few frequent flyer miles, 225,000 to be exact. She uses several different airlines and apparently hadn't used this one in quite some time, which is why she received a note that said, "Upon checking our records, we have found that you haven't flown on one of our flights in 18 months. Therefore, we have removed your miles from your account."

Eileen was incensed. She called the airline and asked if there was a mistake because she had received a letter just three months before that said her miles would expire at the end of December, eight months later. The airline said, "No. It says in your frequent flyer agreement that we can liquidate your miles at any time if we determine that you have not flown with us for awhile." (For those of you who have never read your frequent flyer agreements, they're written in 4-point type. I'm a firm believer that if the print is any smaller than 8-point, it is unreadable and, therefore, doesn't count.)

When the airline sent Eileen the letter informing her that her miles would expire in December, they were setting her expectations. She had the right to expect that she would have her miles until December and that she could use them whenever she wanted before that date. She could use them, not use them, or even save them, but only until the end of December. She could make plans based on what the company promised.

The airline has the right to set deadlines and terms of service. Companies can communicate service level agreements. Deadlines, terms of service and service level agreements create expectations as does marketing. When you violate the expectations you've set, your customers have a right to feel wronged. After all, you made them a promise and told them what to expect.

Word of Mouth
Have you ever heard the same great movie reviews from numerous people? You don't even go to the movies much anymore, but at least five people have told you that a particular movie is terrific. You tell your spouse, "Hey, we really have to see this one!" So you plan to go to the movies on Saturday night. After eating dinner, you head to the theater, full of anticipation.

You sit, poised for a great movie-watching experience. The movie begins. There are a few laughs early, and the characters seem to be fairly likable. But the plot is like one you swear you saw on television and the acting is okay, at best. Still, you think, "The really good part must be coming," and it never does. Two hours later, you walk out of the theater, disappointed.

When you arrive at work on Monday, one of your co-workers asks about your weekend. You tell her you saw this particular movie, and when she asks how you liked it, you reply, "It was good but not nearly as good as everybody said it was. Frankly, I don't know what the big deal was."

Was the movie as bad as you thought? Or were you disappointed because you expected something better? There's a good chance it was the latter.

Your customers talk about you like you talk about movies. Consumers talk to each other all the time about their experiences with different businesses and service providers. If you're in the business-to-business sector, it's likely that your customers know each other or run into each other in various organizations and conferences. If they like you, they'll sing your praises (more on this later). When they sing your praises, the people they're speaking to may decide to do business with you based on the recommendation. The expectation these new customers bring with them comes from what they've heard from others.

They Create Expectations
Combine advertising, branding, promises, what others tell your customers *and* what they remember from the last time they did business with you and you have customer expectations. If I had to ask for a supervisor after being shuttled among three different departments, I'm going to be much more likely to ask for a supervisor after the first transfer next time. Am I being impatient? Yes, because your people tested my patience last time and failed. My expectation is that I will receive the same kind of treatment again, so I'm quick to react.

The converse is also true. If I had an absolutely terrific experience the last time I dealt with your company, well, I'm going to expect to have that experience again. Therefore, I won't be on the offensive the minute I begin talking with you. I will be calmer and willing to let you take your time helping me. If something doesn't seem right, I won't think, "Oh, here we go again" and prepare myself for a horrible experience. I'll have more patience with you.

Our experiences drive our behaviors when dealing with employees and companies because they create expectations.

THE EXPERIENCE BANK ACCOUNT

How do the mind and the heart register this information and make decisions about expectations? When it comes to creating expectations based on previous experiences, we have experience bank accounts.

Some of you may have read about "Emotional Bank Accounts" in Stephen Covey's *Seven Habits of Highly Successful People*. Covey explains the account as "a metaphor that describes the amount of trust that's been built up in a relationship." The Experience Bank Account is similar. Not only does it describe the amount of trust but also what expectations the owner of the account has when it comes to her interactions with you.

I believe that every time we meet people, we open up an account for them. We don't even know we're doing it, but we do it. Inside your experience bank, every person, every business, every organization you've done business with, every school you went to or sent your children to has an account. Those accounts will determine our current and future behavior with these people and organizations.

Say I meet you at a business meeting. We begin chatting and realize we've had a couple of the same clients and know some of the same people. We also find we like to laugh about many of the same things. You have a great sense of humor and I'm funny. As Humphrey Bogart said in *Casablanca*, "I think this is the start of a beautiful friendship."

What you don't realize is you have just opened up a spanking new experience account with "Steve Cohn" written on it. After the meeting, we say goodbye and agree to get together again. You enter your car with a smile on your face and you deposit some points in my account. When you go home, you mention our encounter to your wife and note how great it was. As you do this, you're placing more points in my account.

We agree to get together a few weeks later for coffee at one of the local Starbucks. I offer to pay for the drinks (a few more points in the account), and I come back to the table with your latte and my grande Earl Grey tea. You say, "Today's a tea day?" and I reply, "No, I drink tea all the time. I don't like coffee." You think, *"He doesn't like coffee? What kind of an American is he?"* and you deduct a few points from my account for being a bit strange. We agree to meet for coffee again the next Tuesday morning at 9:30.

Tuesday morning comes and you're at Starbucks again. It's 9:30 and I'm not there. It's 9:45 and I'm not there. Your coffee is getting cold. It's 10:00 and I'm not there. With each 15 minutes, I lose points. You're about to leave and take lots of points out of my account when I show up, apologizing profusely. You forgive me and we have another good conversation, but I lost a bunch of points for being late and not calling.

The next time we get together, I come on time, but not the next time. Or the next time. Or the next time. Each time I show up late, I lose points. And here's the thing about losing points in an experience bank account: if you lose points in consecutive interactions, the number of lost points increases exponentially. I'm teetering on the precipice of your dropping me as a friend if this continues. I have little chance to regain my former high point balance. (For those of you who may have the opportunity to meet me for lunch or coffee/tea, I usually *do* show up on time.)

You've all had that friend who, one day, ran out of points. Yes, she had points once, perhaps lots of points. But experience after experience had reduced the number of points in her account to a minimum. So you started making yourself scarce, turning down invitations to coffee, not calling or not accepting her calls when her name appeared on caller ID. Whether she ran out of points because one bad incident erased them or they disappeared from not being used, she no longer remained in your life. You closed her account.

Think of one of your best friends. You've had so many great experiences with him that he has lots and lots of points in his account. Actually, his account is overflowing with points. You trust him completely because of what's in his experience account. You give him the benefit of the doubt because of what's in his experience account. If he screws up, it's easy for him to apologize because you know he cares about your relationship. More often than not, you're having a good time, not only because you're compatible but also because your expectation was that you would have a good time. The atmosphere is set right from the beginning.

Whether we meet, exceed or don't meet each other's expectations will determine how many points we gain or lose in our experience accounts during each interaction. The longer you're having good experiences with a person, the more you know what to expect, and therefore, the easier it is for him to meet your expectations. Remember, though, the higher the expectations, the higher the rewards (or points), and the lower the expectations, the lower the rewards.

It doesn't matter whether the name on the experience account is an actual person or a company supplying you with the products or services you need. You are always depositing or deducting points in or out of the account. Your customer is doing the same for you.

DO INTERNAL CUSTOMERS HAVE EXPECTATIONS TOO?

The same expectations list we had for our external customers applies to our internal customers. Your co-workers expect you to do what you say you're going to do; show respect, be polite, care, be prompt and on time, show empathy and treat them as people, not as cogs in a wheel. And if there are expectations specific to projects or job responsibilities, we owe it to them and to ourselves to know what they are. If you don't know, ask.

Customer expectations also need to be shared if more than one person is working on the account, which is very often the case. If a client expresses his expectations to the sales representative during the sales process, those expectations must be shared with those who will be involved in any way with the account, including the customer service people, after the sale is closed.

Without the information about these expectations, the other employees cannot manage, meet, or exceed them.

Always Raising the Bar

Since customers have expectations, you can either meet those expectations, exceed those expectations, or fail to meet them. As you'll see when we count down to Chapter 1, there are many ways to exceed expectations once you know what the customer expects. We should all be attempting to exceed expectations as often as we can.

Yet, here's the problem with exceeding expectations – the expectations bar is constantly rising.

My wife and I were driving back to Atlanta from New York where we had been attending a family event. As you might imagine, it's a pretty long drive, so we usually try to stop someplace overnight in Virginia or North Carolina. We hit Virginia before dinnertime and figured we'd stop somewhere in that very large state. However, we quickly found ourselves hungry and in the middle of nowhere. Soon, we started seeing billboards that indicated civilization wasn't too far away.

We pulled off for food at the first exit. As we hit the main street, we noticed several restaurants, none of which were terribly appealing. There were the usual fast food outlets – McDonald's, Burger King, Wendy's – and a local dive called "Bubba and Mama's Rib Joint." When we saw the array of motorcycles in front of the "Joint", we thought it might be a good idea to get back on the highway.

Then we saw a sign for Ponderosa Steakhouse, "steakhouse" being a relative term. Many of you have seen a Ponderosa Steakhouse if not actually eaten in one. It's not bad, especially when the message under the Ponderosa sign says "Sirloin and Buffet $8.99." My wife and I looked at the sign, looked at each other and shrugged our shoulders in a way that said, "Why not? How bad could it be?" (Can you imagine one of your customers saying, "How bad can it be?") We had really low expectations.

When you enter a Ponderosa Steakhouse, you immediately place your order at the counter, usually for steak or chicken. My wife ordered the chicken and I ordered the sirloin. I ordered my steak rare, not expecting that it would be much redder than medium. They handed us two plastic glasses for drinks and a large number stand to place on our table.

Shortly after we sat down, our server came over and introduced herself: "My name is Jasmine, and I'll be your server today. Has anybody told you about the buffet that comes with your meal?"

My wife and I could see the buffet from our table, and frankly, it looked like every other buffet we had seen at low- to medium-priced restaurants. But we played along. Jasmine described the buffet to us:

"You will notice that we have a large bowl of lettuce. Now, for $8.99, you might expect that our lettuce would be wilted, but no. We make sure our lettuce is fresh throughout the day. This also goes for our cucumbers and tomatoes. Our tomatoes are always firm and sweet as are our carrots. In fact, everything on the buffet is fresh and tasty, especially the side dishes. You must try everything you can."

By the time Jasmine had finished describing the buffet, my mouth was watering. So we went up to the buffet. When we came back, Jasmine was back, too, placing our meals on the table. Then she blew me away by asking, "Sir, I want to make sure your steak is as you like it. Can you tell me if it is rare enough for you?" I cut into the steak, and sure enough, it was medium. She said that it was unacceptable for me to eat a steak that did not meet my expectations (don't forget, this was an $8.99 steak that included a buffet), and she took it back to the kitchen. I don't see that kind of service in top restaurants.

Jasmine brought a new steak, apologized once again for the condition of the last one and asked if she could do anything else. We said no and proceeded to eat our meals (with the fresh food from the buffet!). As we were finishing our meal, Jasmine arrived again.

"Have you considered our dessert buffet? We've got chocolate and vanilla ice cream and you are really cheating yourself if you don't try our chocolate pudding. It's the best chocolate pudding in Virginia." I peeked over at the chocolate pudding and I could swear it was the same as the pudding cups my daughters took to school for lunch, but I let her continue. She was so excited that I thought she would burst.

After dessert, Jasmine came back one more time. I complimented her on the wonderful experience we had because she had been such a good server. I told her I wished I knew people in the area because I would recommend her. She said that it wasn't necessary; she just loved to serve people. We got back on the road, but we didn't stop talking about Jasmine for quite some time.

When I walked into that Ponderosa Steakhouse, my expectations were extremely low. For $8.99, I expected an $8.99 steak, if you know what I mean. I received so much more, mainly because of the experience I received at Jasmine's table. The taste of the food met my expectations – it was okay and not much more. But Jasmine's service was through the roof.

Jasmine far exceeded my expectations, so what happens now?

1. If I'm ever in that town in Virginia, I'm going to stop at that Ponderosa Steakhouse.
2. The reputation of every Ponderosa Steakhouse in the U.S. went up based on my experience at that particular Ponderosa.
3. Because the reputation of Ponderosa Steakhouse went up, my expectations will be higher if I go to another one.

I have to admit that my experience with Jasmine's service has made it much more possible that I'll stop at a Ponderosa again, but they'll have a pretty high expectation to meet. My expectations for Ponderosa will never be as low again as they were that day.

Expectations drive everything, from your business relationships to your personal ones. They drive your customers to your business and can drive them away if you don't meet or exceed them.

It's not rocket service.

Rocket Review

Everything is about expectations.

- High expectations = High rewards and Low expectations = Low rewards.
- Expectations are not right or wrong, good or bad. They just are.
- If you do what the customer expects, you're nothing special.
- Experiences determine customer expectations and vice versa.
- Each time we meet somebody, they open an experience account with our name on it.
- When you exceed expectations, you raise the bar for the next time.

Manager Lift-Off

If expectations determine how our customers feel before, during and after interactions with us, they also determine whether our customers continue to do business with us. Once again, it doesn't take a rocket scientist to realize that we'd better know our customers' expectations.

A few years ago, I worked for a major high-end product company who hired me to help them encourage the retail store salespeople to sell more of their product. They asked me to speak at their annual sales meeting in Las Vegas.

First, I interviewed several company representatives. I asked them for information about the store salespeople and what would make those salespeople sell more of the product. I wanted to create a benchmark to work from. Part of what I wanted to know was what those salespeople's expectations were. The company reps had never considered that they needed to know such a thing. I then called several storeowners and managers who carried the company's products. The remarkable result was that the answers from the latter group were different from the former. The store owners and managers had a completely different perception of why a store salesperson chooses to sell a company's products than did the company's reps. The most interesting answers revolved around expectations.

"When the company rep comes into the store, he tends to talk with the owner or the manager. He'll engage us and sometimes wine and dine us. He rarely talks to the floor salespeople. We [the owners and managers] already know him. We like his products," said one storeowner.

Sadly, he added, the salespeople know how the rep behaves and therefore don't expect him to talk to them. All the rep has to do to exceed their expectations is to talk to them and show them some attention. If he were to show the salespeople attention and exceed their expectations, they'll show his product first and with enthusiasm.

For years, this company's sales force had decided what the customer's expectations were without ever asking the customer. Every company, department, regional office, manager or employee should know the customer's expectations from the customer's point of view. How do we find out the customer's point of view? We ask.

We should be asking the customer about his or her expectations regularly – once a year or more. Questions could include some of the following:

- What are 5 or 10 expectations you have of your sales representative?
- What do you expect when you call customer service?
- What kind of time expectations do you have when it comes to emergencies?
- What do you expect when you open a new account with us?
- What do you expect after the job is done?
- What kind of follow-up do you expect?
- How often do you expect us to keep in touch during a project?
- What will make this project, training, product, or event successful for you?
- What kind of information do you expect from us?

Additional questions should deal with particular issues depending on the product, service, company and situation.

Once you have gathered the information from these questions about expectations, you and your people should get together and brainstorm and ask these questions:

- How can we meet these expectations?
- Who is responsible for each of these expectations? How can I help if I am not the one responsible?
- What resources are needed to meet each of these expectations?
- Are these expectations reasonable? If not, how can we reset the expectations so the customer is on the same page as we are?
- Once we've determined how to meet each of these expectations, how do we exceed them?

It is very rare for an employee to take the kind of initiative to determine the customer's expectations and then meet or exceed them. More often than not, the employee will take his or her cue from you.

The first expectation most employees strive to meet is the manager's. People will do what you pay them to do. Before they determine what the customer wants and expects, they want to know what you expect. A wise person once told me, "Find out what the boss wants, and give it to him. That's the secret of success."

However, be aware of communicating conflicting expectations. Be sure your people know what you expect of them in clear and simple terms. There should never be confusion around expectations, both yours and the customer's. Once you know the customer's expectations, the rest is simple.

It's not rocket service.

COUNTDOWN:

R-E-S-P-E-C-T

Growing up in my grandfather's store, I saw up close the impact of human contact in business. Mac's Men's Shop was a hands-on business, a place where people came in to shop, buy, and schmooze with Grandpa Max and my father. It was more than a transaction. There was little self-service. Sure, a customer could pick a tie off the rack or grab some socks and underwear from the display, but on the whole, you had to interact with somebody.

This was not only true in retail establishments. As recently as the first years of the 21st century, you could still go to a storefront to pay your utility bill. It was not that many years ago when you would always talk to a human being when calling a company. At the very least, you talked to a switchboard operator.

The world has changed, and I believe for the better. Surveys show that most people prefer to use an ATM to deposit and withdraw cash from their accounts, shop in big box stores where they exchange hands-on service for extensive selection, leave voicemail rather than depending on someone forwarding a message, and in increasing numbers, shop online for items they used to need a local store to carry. Even in business-to-business transactions, the days of the "travelling salesman" or "outside product representative" is disappearing rapidly, and companies procure items directly online.

Yet people tell me all the time that they are thirsty for human contact in business. *It's not rocket service.* We all know what we like in interacting with companies. Despite all the convenience of self-service and ease of purchase online, people wish they had a human being to talk to when they have a problem or a question. If I had a dollar for every time somebody said to me, "I wish I could talk to a real person once in awhile instead of a) hearing a recording that says, 'Your call is very important to us'; b) hitting this prompt or that prompt; c) leaving a voice message; or d) answering questions by pressing this key or that" I'd be a rich man.

Therefore, organizations need to balance self-service, which provides convenience to the customer and cost savings to the company, and providing human contact, which costs more in labor but satisfies our urge to talk to a human being.

Self-service is not going away, nor should it. But when self-service, prompts, or FAQs are insufficient for dealing with customers who want reassurance, are emotional, or have numerous questions, a real person needs to take care of the situation. How well they do so begins with how well they provide respect.

Ways to Show Respect

One of the most important skills in interacting with customers is understanding what they need (as opposed to what they want). Customers have needs – physical, substantial, and emotional. When you know what their needs are, you can do something to make them happy.

The first and most important need is the need for respect. Customers are handing over their hard-earned money to you. They have made a choice to do business with you, usually over somebody else. They deserve your respect.

What kinds of things can we do to show our customers respect?

I ask this question in every class. The participants in the class are very quick to answer, and whether or not they actually do these things, their answers are right on target. Here are some of the things that usually come up:

- Treat people as unique individuals.
- Acknowledge their specific and unique needs and challenges.
- Use the customer's name.
- Give your total attention.

Treat People as Unique Individuals

There was a Bugs Bunny cartoon (yes, I am using Bugs Bunny as a reference for this book!) during which Bugs does something to make Elmer Fudd look bad, as usual. Suddenly, Elmer turns into a lollypop with the word "sucker" on the large round part. Sometimes I think that while we don't look at our customers as "suckers" we do look at them as "dollar signs." You're Bugs offering Elmer a product or service, and before he even says a word, you're seeing him as a giant dollar sign. Salespeople are notorious for this, counting the money they will make from a customer before the sale is even complete. We've all experienced feeling as if a salesperson saw us as a dollar sign rather than as a person.

The customer is not an account number. He is not an object. He is not a problem or the problem he is calling about. He is not the sum of his purchases, service calls, and money spent.

When I was a teenager, I worked in a catering hall as a bus boy. It was a pretty good job for a 17 year old. What 17 year old doesn't want to go to a party each week and get paid for it? I set up the tables and brought the salads and dinners for the wedding and bar mitzvah attendees. It was cool.

The first party I worked was a wonder to behold. There was the lothario at table 3 who monopolized the dance floor, and the young couple at table 5 who couldn't keep their eyes off each other. The tall guy with the blonde hair at table 6 was cracking everybody up, and the loud guy at table 10 was making obscene jokes about my pepper grinder. All in all, it was a colorful evening with clear personalities at each of the tables.

The next week, I worked another party and noticed similar people but not with the clarity I had during the first party. As the weeks and months went on, sadly one party flowed into the next until they all became one big blur. Each was just another event. I no longer noticed – or remembered – the individuals at the parties. They were just new faces in the same seats and would be replaced with more new people the next week. They were no longer individuals; they were just attendees. There was nothing unique or memorable about them.

Are your customers and their issues one big blur? Have you begun to treat them all the same – as just another customer? Or do you see each customer as unique?

Acknowledge Their Specific and Unique Needs and Challenges
Treat customers as individuals with individual and unique wants and needs. Each customer is unique. Each person is unique. You may have heard this situation or problem 489 times before, but it's the first time it's happened to her. It may seem remarkably simple or it may even seem like no big deal to you, but it's a big deal to her. It's not so simple for the customer when she can't figure it out.

Part of treating a customer as unique is focusing on the person, not on the procedure. A number of years ago, we found out my daughter needed jaw surgery. We found out about the need for the surgery in March, and the doctor, who saw my daughter as a teenager, offered to arrange to perform the surgery in June so that Ariel would be healed by the time school started in August. He knew middle school students can be cruel, especially when your jaw is wired shut and you can't talk or eat properly.

The insurance company didn't share our concerns. Despite our begging to speed up the approval process (which really shouldn't have taken that long), they finally approved my daughter's surgery for early August, leaving her to begin 8th grade with her jaw wired shut and all the cruelty that came with it. Now an adult, my daughter still talks about the emotional pain of that experience – as if it were yesterday.

Patients are people first. Health is the most personal thing people have and when it's in jeopardy, they are vulnerable and scared. They are not the sum of their symptoms. They are the sum of their emotions, wants, needs, desires, *and* their symptoms.

Customers are not dollar signs. They are people with individual wants, needs, and situations. When we deal with people every day, our customers can become one big blur. After a while, they're no longer people; they're just the problems we have to fix. We have to be careful, though, not to allow that to happen.

In the end, customers will make decisions about you based on how personal your service is and how unique they feel. If they feel like a number, they won't be happy. If they feel like you don't care, they won't be happy. If they feel like you're not creating a solution with their needs in mind, they won't be happy.

It's not rocket service.

Each customer has certain needs. He may have the same needs as many of your other customers. But to him, nobody else has ever had the same needs for the same reasons in the same way. Acknowledge this when you deal with your customers. You'll be glad you did.

Use the Customer's Name

When recently working with a major healthcare system, a woman said to me, "Oh let me tell you a story about what happened to me! I had just had eye surgery and went to my post operation check up a few weeks later. When the doctor came in the room, he walked right over to me, bent down and looked straight into my repaired eye. He never said 'hello' or 'how are you feeling?' He never addressed me by my name. He just looked at my eye, twisting his head from right to left and up and down. Then, after he finished, he finally spoke to me. Why would a doctor do that?" I answered, "Because you were an 'eye.' You didn't have a name. You weren't a person. You were an operation. As far as he was concerned, he operated on your eye, not on you. You just happened to be attached to your eye. He cared about the eye, not you."

Customers have names. Ask a customer for his name and use it. Before you start solving the problem, doing your research, or identifying the situation, say his name. Doing so says, "I know you are a human being, not an account number. You are unlike any other customer in the world. Your name is ..."

After you use his name, use yours. If using his name says, "You're a person," using your name says, "I'm a person talking to a person. I'm not a nameless, faceless company talking to an account number." Suddenly, there's a human element that didn't exist before. Before you answered his call, all you were was a telephone number, infused with all the negative experiences he has had with service or product problems. When you say your name, you are communicating that you are an individual, not the last person he spoke with or even the person before that.

When you say your name, make sure the other person can understand it. I recently called a customer service department, and the person who answered said something that sounded like this: "Welcome to Acme Corporation, my name is mrrhy. HowmayIhelpyou?" She said her name in such a muffled and quick way that I couldn't tell what it was. Was her name Mary or Murphy or Mommy or...Mrrhy? Whatever it was, I couldn't understand her. Say your name like you're proud of it.

Names are so important. Next time you go into a restaurant and the server says, "Hi, my name is Lucia. I'll be your server today," respond with, "Hi Lucia." And then when you have a question about something on the menu, say, "Lucia, can you tell me if the lemon in the chicken piccata is overwhelming?" Use her name and she will give you great service.

Give Your Total Attention

Your current customer is the only customer in the world at this moment. He deserves your total attention. He should never get the feeling that you are looking at something else, talking to somebody else, or thinking about something other than him.

I remember a phone conversation from a number of years ago that I had with my younger daughter. She was about 11 or 12 years old and I was calling from the road. My wife handed her the phone and our conversation went something like this:

"Hi, Hannah."

"Hi, Daddy."

"Whatcha doing?"

(silence)

"Whatcha doing? Hannah?"

(distracted) "What?

"Whatcha doing?

"Oh ... nothing."

"Nothing? You must be doing something."

(silence)

"Hannah?"

"What?"

"What are you watching on TV?"

Now, why would I think she was watching TV? Well, first, I knew that when she watched TV she went into a catatonic state. But most importantly, I knew she wasn't paying attention to me, so she must have been paying attention to something else. (She's all grown up now and we have good conversations ... unless she's on Facebook.)

Your customer knows when you're paying attention to something else, even if your interaction is online. In an online customer service chat, you enter the chat room and wait until the customer service representative writes, "Hi. I'm Melinda and I will be happy to be your consultant today." You write, "Hi, Melinda." Then you wait 90 seconds or so and finally Melinda responds, "What can I do for you today?" You explain your problem and then you wait ... and wait ... and wait until she responds, "I'll be happy to help you today. May I have your account number?"

Did it really take her up to 2 minutes to come up with "I'll be happy to help you today?" No! She was likely trying to assist more than one customer at a time. While you were waiting for her answer, she was helping someone else and not paying attention to you.

OTHER BASIC CUSTOMER NEEDS

Customers have several other basic needs and respect is a major part of each of them.

Constant Communication

You call the help desk because your computer is stalling and rebooting without any explanation. The help desk technician walks you through a process that seems to right the situation. But the next day, it happens again. So you call the help desk for a second time.

A female voice answers the phone. She says, "My name is Cindy. How may I help you?" You explain that the same thing that happened yesterday is happening today and you're becoming frantic. At that moment, she asks, "What is your account number?" even though you had punched it in just a few minutes earlier in response to the Interactive Voice Response (IVR) recording. You tell her and then ...

Nothing.

You hear a keyboard being tapped in the background, but you don't hear Cindy. She's not saying anything. Still, you wait for what seems like minutes until she comes back and says, "Okay, so what seems to be the issue?"

You had already told her but now have to tell her again, at which point she says, "Just a minute."

Silence.

Silence.

And more silence.

Then she takes a deep sigh and you want to jump through the phone!

Wouldn't it be better if it sounded like this?

A female voice answers the phone. She says, "My name is Cindy. How may I help you?" You explain that the same thing that happened yesterday is happening today and you're becoming frantic. At that moment, she says, "I'm sorry, but I need to ask for your account number again. The number you entered was just to get you to the right person. I don't have the number in front of me."

Knowing the reason, you repeat the number. She says, "Thank you. I'm going to bring up your account to see what we've done before. Give me about 30 seconds."

During that 30 seconds she says, "I'm awfully sorry this happened. I'm also sorry that my computer seems to be moving a little slow. It'll just be a little longer until it comes up on the screen. Oh! There it is. Now, let's take a look at this."

She's been doing several things since answering the phone, but has not stopped keeping you informed. After about 10 seconds, she says, "Okay, I see you called yesterday but apparently, the same thing is happening again today, is that correct?" You confirm her statement and then she says, "Let me do some quick research to see what might be happening here."

While she looks, she continues to tell you what is on the screen, so much so that you feel you are sitting right next to her. Then, suddenly, she sighs and says, "I think I know what the problem is. Here's what I found …"

Not once during the entire conversation did you feel she had left you or was helping somebody else. There was no silence, no pauses, no keyboard tapping, no nothing.

When working with customers, it is important to keep them informed as often as possible. If you're on the phone, let them know what you're doing as you're doing it. If you're not able to be on the phone with them during the process, send updates regularly. What's regularly? Ask your customers. Their interpretation of regularly may be different than yours. If they send you an email asking for something or giving you information you need to help them, respond with a confirmation email.

Never assume the person who sent you the email knows you're working on the problem. Joe gets an email from Susan asking for his help on a project and Joe immediately begins working on it. He's a good partner. He's very conscientious. He's getting the job done. But Susan doesn't know!

On the other end of the email, Susan wonders if Joe even received her email. Of course, Susan can put a received notification on the email so she knows Joe did receive it. Yet even with a receipt, Susan doesn't know if Joe is working on the project. She doesn't know where he is in the process. She doesn't know when it will be done. She doesn't know anything more than the fact that Joe received her email.

When somebody sends an email with a request, take a moment and reply. Even if you can't work on the request right now, you can send a reply that says, "Hi Susan, I received your email and I will work on it this afternoon. I'll keep you posted on my progress." By doing this, you're setting expectations.

This will make Susan happy, even though you're not dropping everything else you're working on. Most times, people just want to know the status of a project so they can plan accordingly.

When a customer needs you to do something and is concerned about whether it's going to be done or not, silence is lethal. Silence is frustrating and grates on the nerves. She can't see you, she can't hear you, she doesn't know what you are or aren't doing. All she knows is her problem still exists. You may be sweating and working diligently, but she doesn't know. Don't assume she knows you're working on it. She doesn't assume anything because of the lousy customer service she's received in the past (whether by you or someone else).

Think of it this way: if your customer were standing in front of you while you worked on her situation, she would know everything. But what if your customer were blind? What if she couldn't see you? Would you let her just stand there while you worked? Or would you tell her what you're doing so she doesn't feel so impatient, nervous and ... blind?

Your customers are in the dark. They don't know your job. They don't know what you can do. They can't see any progress you are or aren't making. They need you to tell them what's going on. If you keep them posted, they will remain calm, their blood pressure won't rise, and they will be more apt to give you the benefit of the doubt.

Treat your customers as if they were blind because, in many ways, they are.

Know What's Coming Next
You know what the environment is. You know how long it will take and the obstacles you may encounter. You know how complicated the problem is or isn't. Since you know these things, you owe it to your customers to communicate it to them.

Knowing what's coming is a basic human need. That's why we watch the weather on TV. That's why sports fans watch pre-game shows.

When we know what's coming, we can plan. We can bring an umbrella if we know it's going to rain. We can make changes to our fantasy sports team because we found out one of our players is hurt.

When people know what's going on, they are more at ease.

It's not rocket service.

Feel in Control
Customers have a need to feel in control. You have the products, you have the answers, you have the processes and they only have their situations. Find ways to help the customer feel in control.

For instance, when you can, give the customer options. Customers love options. Having options makes them feel in control.

Several years ago, I had surgery on my right shoulder. After having an MRI on the bad shoulder, I went to my doctor. He said, "I've looked at your MRI and you have three muscle tears in your shoulder. We can do one of two things: We can do surgery on the shoulder now, or I can send you to physical therapy for about six months, after which you'll more than likely still need surgery. Which option would you like to do?"

It didn't take me long to say, "Let's do the surgery now."

The doctor replied, "Good choice!"

The doctor gave me options. He put me in control. I made my own decision on my health and my body. He made me feel that I was in control and had made the right choice.

Here's the good news about giving customers options. You make them feel in control even though you are still in control. You're the one who came up with the options. More than likely, you explained the pros and cons of the options. The information the customer is acting on came from you. However, the customer doesn't realize that. It's a win-win.

Reassurance

Customers need assurance and reassurance. They need to feel they are doing the right thing and that you are doing the right thing. It doesn't take very long to say, "It's going to be all right" or "This won't take too long." Of course, make sure you don't say something just to make them feel good, even though you know it's not or may not be true. We've all had the experience of a healthcare provider saying, "This won't hurt a bit" right before you scream out in pain!

Trust in You

Customers need to trust you. Don't assume that the customer trusts you from the start. You have to earn the customer's trust through the work you do, the words you say, and the results you produce. When customers trust you, they are less likely to get upset, scream, yell, or be difficult. We'll talk quite a bit about the things you can do to gain your customer's trust in the next few chapters.

Flexibility

Customers need you to be flexible. Not every situation is the same. Not every problem has the same details or solutions. To treat customers as unique individuals, you need to provide flexibility based on their unique needs and situations. If you're not flexible, I might as well be talking to a machine. Being flexible is not only good for the customer, it's good for you. When we are too set in our ways or too tied to specific rules and outcomes, we are bound to become frustrated and sadly, take it out on the customer or on our co-workers. I subscribe to the credo, "Blessed are those who are flexible. They shall never be bent out of shape." (Should the customer be flexible too? Perhaps. But as I said before, it begins with you.)

It Doesn't Have to Cost Anything

If you'll notice, none of these needs cost you, the company or service provider any money. Even "doing more than what is expected" doesn't necessarily mean you have to give something away that you would normally charge for. None of these things will cause you to lose money. And if you think these needs will cause you to lose time, just think of the amount of time you'll be spending dealing with this customer when he or she becomes upset or angry because you didn't meet these needs. As the late, great UCLA basketball Coach John Wooden said, "If you don't have time to do it right, when will you have time to do it over?"

Customers have a need for respect. Whether they deserve your respect or not (based on previous experiences), they still have a need for it. They will penalize you if you do not respect them.

It's not rocket service.

Rocket Review

- All customers need respect. They are not numbers, body parts, or the sum of all of their purchases. They are not problems or issues; they are people.

- Acknowledge that each customer is unique. They want you to consider them as individuals with individual wants, needs and situations.

- When you use the customer's name, you're saying, "You're a person, an individual. And I respect that." When you use your name, you're saying, "I'm a person talking to a person and not a faceless company talking to an account number or a problem."

- Give the customer your total attention and provide constant communication.

- Let customers know what's coming. Let them know what to expect. Keep them feeling safe and in control. Give them options.

- Customers need to trust you. When they trust you, they will more likely accept your explanations, questions and solutions.

- Be as flexible as you can be. The more the customer feels you are flexible, the happier they will be and the easier they will be to work with.

Manager Lift-Off

A client of mine did something interesting. She invited a major customer to come to her company's annual management retreat. After my client showered her customer with wonderful words about how much she enjoyed working with him, she gave him the floor. He returned the favor, saying how much he liked working with her group.

He then took questions from the group, with the understanding that his answers would be completely honest. "Don't ask me a question if you don't want to hear an honest answer," he said. "Of course, if you don't ask the question, you'll never know how I feel or what I need."

What followed was an honest, open discussion about both companies and what they could do to make their relationship better. Both parties walked away with a greater understanding. What are you doing to make sure your people have a better understanding of their customers' needs and expectations?

Perhaps you can invite a major customer to do exactly what this customer did. I'm sure most of your customers wouldn't open themselves up to such a situation but many will. When your people can put a face with the name or the company and can hear honest feedback, not from you but from the customer, they will be more likely to treat the customer with the respect and attention the customer deserves.

As I said in the last chapter, you can't know what your customers' expectations are unless you ask. The same applies to their needs. A relationship, personal or professional, takes two people. If the only thing that connects you to your customer is the product you provide, then the relationship will be about products. And when your customer finds a product that is better or cheaper than yours, the relationship will dissipate.

We talked quite a lot about respect in this chapter. How are you doing in that area with your employees? One of the complaints that comes up in survey after survey of employee/manager relationships is "lack of respect" – from both sides. As the established professional in the employee/manager relationship, you need to treat your people respectfully even if they don't treat you with the same regard. In return, they will respect you.

Employees, like external customers, want and need respect. Give them the respect they need, and they will go to the wall for you.

COUNTDOWN:

Helplessness is Your Customer's Fuse

Did you ever have that dream where you can't move? You try to call out for help but no sound comes out of your mouth? Or even if you can make a sound, nobody seems to hear you? A dream like that will jar you right out of your sleep.

It's a scary thought, not having anybody hear you. If no one can hear you, then no one can help you. If no one can help you, well, then you're doomed! It's enough to give you nightmares.

Welcome to the world of your customer.

Customers get angry, customers get upset, customers lash out. They yell. They scream. They cry. They go away and don't come back. Why do customers scream and yell when they feel wronged? Why do they lash out? Because they don't believe anybody cares about them. In other words, they feel helpless. It's like they're in that dream all over again.

Why do they feel helpless? Because they've been in this situation before and have been met with disinterest, a lack of empathy, and people who just didn't give a damn. So when we're thinking, "Why are they being so difficult?" the difficulty often is us.

<h1 style="text-align:center">%&*%&*&*#$*(#!!!</h1>

She wasn't a ticking time bomb when she first called your company or entered the store. She just wanted somebody to help her. She always prided herself as someone who could stay calm in a crisis, as an understanding friend who gives people the benefit of the doubt. She had "nice" written all over her face. But then it all became too difficult. She asked for a supervisor, but none of the supervisors were around. She looked at the frequently asked questions online or at the troubleshooting guide in the manual and still couldn't figure it out. She felt helpless. And then she spoke to you.

When the customer feels helpless, she doesn't know where to turn or what to do. You are all that stands between her and her uncontrollable inclination to explode. You are the explosives expert who has to pull the correct wire to defuse the bomb. If you move it the right way, use gentle effort, and pull just at the exact time, everybody is safe and all is quiet. However, if you use the wrong technique – KABOOM!

Your customer's helplessness is the fuse. The more helpless she feels, the shorter her fuse. You may have arrived just as the fuse was about to reach the point of explosion. It doesn't matter if you lit the fuse or if you caused the fuse to burn to this point. You have to put out the fire. One false step and your customer explodes.

Difficult customers aren't necessarily difficult people. The reverse may be true (difficult people *are* difficult customers), but a majority of your customers don't naturally display any of those horrible traits I described earlier. Most of your customers are not difficult people to start with. They just want something done. Many times, there's a valid reason they've become upset.

ONLY ONE REASON THEY GET UPSET

Anybody who has spent more than a day with me knows I am a HUGE baseball fan. From mid-November until late-March, the priorities in my life are in the following order: my wife, my kids, my business, the rest of my family, my friends, and then everybody else.

From that March or April day when the first pitch of the season is thrown, these are my priorities: my wife, my kids, BASEBALL, my business, the rest of my family, my friends, and then everybody else. (My wife and kids made me write it in this order.) So, suffice it to say, if anything gets in the way of baseball, it is a major crisis in my life.

November 4, 2001 was one of those days. The Arizona Diamondbacks and the New York Yankees were to play in the seventh and final game of that year's World Series. The series was tied 3-3 and the games had been incredibly exciting.

I was especially interested in this series because I have a particular dislike for the New York Yankees. Growing up in New York, you're either a Yankees fan or a Mets fan. You can't be both. It would be like having two religions or two spouses. Through three generations, my family cast its lot with the Mets. To see those hated Yankees lose the World Series would make my year.

The morning of Game 7, one of my daughters informed me that the cable was "out" on our TV. I checked the TV, confirmed her observation, and called the cable company.

"I'd like to report that my cable is out and I need it fixed today. It's very important," I said calmly.

"We can have somebody out there Wednesday."

"Wednesday? No, I need somebody here today," I said with more concern in my voice.

"I'm sorry, sir. We don't have anybody available 'til Wednesday."

I tried to sound nice and pleasant, but firm. "You don't understand. It's an emergency. Tonight is the seventh game of the World Series, and I have no cable."

This woman had no empathy for me (or sympathy, for that matter). "We'll be able to get somebody out there Wednesday."

Now I was getting desperate. "But I'm having 10 people over

tonight to watch the game, and my wife has made 3 dishes, and I have no cable!" (I made that up but figured it was worth a shot.)

"Sir, all the appointments are taken for today. Your technician will come Wednesday and we will credit you for three days without cable."

"You will credit me for the three days?" I said louder, feeling more and more helpless. "What does that mean?"

"You will get three days' credit for not having service. That's what we're required to do."

"Three days? I don't pay for cable by the day! I pay for a month of cable. If I don't get a month of cable, I should get a month free! Especially when I'm missing the seventh game of the World Series!"

Now I was speaking very loudly. Why? Because I felt helpless. In her mind, it didn't matter if it was the seventh game of the World Series, the night of the Oscars, the moon landing, or the day the world was ending. Nothing was going to change the schedule.

To her, this conversation was not about me. It was about her. It was about the cable company. It was about what she was required to do – and what she wasn't required to do.

She didn't feel my pain. She didn't empathize. She didn't sympathize. She didn't care. I was just another customer with another complaint.

A baseball fanatic with a World Series obsession?

"Not my problem."

I could have screamed. I could have cried. But I didn't. I called the satellite TV company.

In the end, she may have been telling the truth; she really couldn't do anything for me. There really wasn't anybody available that day. But I didn't feel that she was spending any time or thought trying to figure out if there was a way to make it happen. She knew what she could do and couldn't step out of her box. For all I know, she was afraid to do so because there may have been consequences for her and if that were the case, both she and I were victims of this situation.

Still, my concern was not whether she needed to follow procedure. My concern was with my World Series game. That's all.

The thing about helpless customers is they're not really helpless. They only feel helpless. Once they gather their thoughts, they find alternatives that include, more often than not, going to your competitor. Or making a video on YouTube.

As I was sitting on my couch, talking to a CSR who had no power to do anything, I felt helpless. It's the only reason customers get upset.

Sure, we could list all the reasons we think customers get upset. We could list all the reasons they've been nasty, obnoxious, arrogant, and, in rare cases, violent. We could list all the reasons they become snide, condescending, and demanding. But all of those reasons fall under the same category: helplessness.

When you're transferred three times and then cut off, you become upset because you feel helpless.

When you call the insurance company for the third time to find out why you haven't been paid and they tell you they can't find your claim, you feel helpless.

When you can't understand the representative based in a foreign country who insists that he doesn't need to transfer you to someone you can understand better, you feel helpless.

When in the middle of your telling your tale to the service desk employee, he interrupts you to answer a phone call, and then is on the phone for almost 10 minutes while you stand there, you feel helpless.

When the technology company continues to tell you how to fix your service yet their solution doesn't work, you feel helpless.

When you hear "There's nothing we can do," you feel worse than helpless.

You get my drift.

It's not rocket service.

They Can Talk About You from Anywhere

When customers feel helpless, they become upset. Upset customers are more dangerous than ever. A woman in Portland, Oregon rides her bicycle into the drive-thru lane at a local fast-food hamburger establishment. The teen-aged employee at the window tells her she can't use the drive-thru because she is "driving" a *bicycle*. When she protests to the manager, he says the same thing and tells her to ride her bicycle to the front of the restaurant and come in through the front doors. She is hungry and figures she is there already, so she complies.

However, she does something before coming into the restaurant. As she gets off her bicycle, she pulls out her smartphone and goes on Twitter, where she has approximately 1,500 followers. Our heroine is not only a bicycle enthusiast, but she is also a bicycle advocate, the kind who advocate for bike lanes and the like.

As her 1,500 followers receive her "tweet," they, in turn, "re-tweet" to their followers, which, if you do the math, probably numbered in the hundreds of thousands (assuming each follower has at least 100 unique followers). Before the end of the day, a local radio talk show host hears about the woman's experience and puts her on the show to talk about it – where she names the restaurant and the location.

Singing a Helpless Tune

Up until 2008, United Airlines (now United Continental) was known for being one of the leading airlines in the world. Depending on the year (and the most recent industry mergers), United often carried more passengers than any other U.S. airline. Its advertising was ubiquitous and with a classically large public relations arm, it basically controlled what the public heard or knew about it.

Then came Dave Carroll, a Canadian country singer and musician who was traveling on United with his band, Sons of Maxwell. Carroll and the band watched helplessly as United bag handlers mishandled their instruments. I'll let Carroll pick up the story from here:

"In the spring of 2008, Sons of Maxwell were traveling to Nebraska for a one-week tour and my Taylor guitar was witnessed being thrown by United Airlines baggage handlers in Chicago. I discovered later that the $3500 guitar was severely damaged. They didn't deny the experience occurred, but for nine months, the various people I communicated with put the responsibility for dealing with the damage on everyone other than themselves, and finally said they would do nothing to compensate me for my loss. So I promised the last person to finally say 'no' to compensation (Ms. Irlweg) that I would write and produce three songs about my experience with United Airlines and make videos for each to be viewed online by anyone in the world."

The "United Breaks Guitars" video, featuring Carroll and the band singing an amusing but biting song detailing the incident, had been accessed more than 10 million times on YouTube as of late 2010. It scored mentions and stories from virtually every major news organization in the United States and elsewhere. Carroll's two additional videos on the subject also received great attention. Suffice it to say, United has been scrambling to manage the damage ever since.

What are your customers saying about you?

Twitter, Facebook, websites, smartphones that record video, and split-second technology have enabled angry customers to tell the *world* about your company and your performance. And don't think you're protected just because you're a CSR answering the phones. People will not only name the company and product, but they'll name the individual employees they dealt with. Dave Carroll mentioned the United customer service person in his song, giving her a place in the customer service "hall of infamy" forever. The next time an angry customer says, "Can I get your name?" watch out.

The worst part about it is that customers can do this while they are still red-hot and steaming over what happened. It used to be that you would have a bad customer experience and you'd have to come home and write a letter to complain about it. By the time you did that or spoke to friends about the incident, chances are you would have cooled off. Now there's no cooling off period.

In the American Express survey I mentioned in the introduction:

- 48% use online postings or blogs to get others' opinions about how companies treat their customers.
- 57% put more emphasis on negative blog and social networking reviews than on positive ones.

It is more important than ever to find a way to diffuse and take care of difficult situations.

NOT ALL CUSTOMERS ARE CREATED EQUAL

Before I start talking about how to deal with difficult customers, let's first talk about a growing movement within customer care that is very positive and can go a long way towards reducing the number of abusive, serial callers. Many companies are finding it in their interest, their employees' interest, and in the interest of their better customers to jettison the abusive customers from their customer lists. Sometimes, it's best just to let the bad ones go.

This is something that is an organization and management issue. The CSR or technician on the line really can't establish this policy and process. This needs to be an organizational initiative to differentiate between different customers based on their purchasing frequency, their potential for more business, the way they treat your employees and the amount of effort and time it takes to make them happy.

A customer who consistently purchases more, has been doing it for years and is very profitable, gets the most points in this process. This is our golden customer. We will pull out the stops for this one, and if there is a rule that can be bent, this is the customer you do it for most frequently. We put our best people on her account. There is no clock or time limit for talking with this customer. This customer's interactions aren't even counted in the average handle time measurement.

I had a client who complained that a certain representative spends too much time talking with the customers. She told me, "She's very good at solving problems and the customers love her. But she stays on the phone too damn long! What should I do with her?" I replied,

"Put her with your best customers. If she's good at customer care and loves to establish relationships and not transactions, your best customers deserve the attention."

Just below this category of customer are those who purchase less but purchase more profitable items, those who are growing companies with great potential for business, and those who have gone out of their way to spread your name to others positively.

Some companies have added another category for customers who aren't very profitable or large purchasers but still want this high level of service. These customers can purchase a plan that will give it to them. They haven't earned it but pay for it. (I'm one of these customers. Since I only buy a couple of computers from my computer company during a three-year-period, I don't fit into a "favored client" category. But I still want that kind of service. So I pay a fee to receive the kind of service they usually reserve for their best customers. It's fair.)

The customers who call all the time, who are constantly demanding your attention, and who are known for abusing your people are those who fall into the category of "unwanted." Often, these customers are those who got coerced into buying your product or did so on a spur of the moment decision and then regret the purchase. These are the ones you can never satisfy, no matter what you do.

These customers are often not worth having. Even if they contribute a high level of purchases, you have to consider letting them go. If they are not profitable or are barely profitable, they need to be shown the door. These customers are using resources that you can use for better, more profitable, and less demanding customers. You should not waste your time on them. Give them back their money and send them to the competition, where you win twice. They are out of your hair and in your competition's – absorbing *their* resources.

Companies who have established such categories can easily say, "We don't want you as a customer anymore. You abuse our people. You don't treat us with respect and you take up time and resources we could be using for customers who don't do that. The level of business we do with you doesn't justify the time and effort we're putting into your account. And even if you did do an enormous amount of business with us, we will not tolerate anybody abusing our employees who are doing their best to help."

Once you get rid of the consistently abusive customers, you can focus on the difficult ones. There will still be those who abuse, but they will be rare.

How Do We Deal With It?

So how do we deal with these difficult customers? First of all, we acknowledge to ourselves that something has made them this upset and it's not their fault they're behaving this way. There are people in this world who are downright mean and nasty, but most of your customers begin their conversations with you with good intentions.

We know this instinctively. *It's not rocket service.*

Remember, solving customer problems is about *them*, not you. Customers' screaming is not about *you*. Customers' throwing things is not about *you*. Whatever is going on, don't take it personally. Keep the focus on them because their anger isn't about you.

We don't have to get down in the dirt with an angry and abusive customer. We don't have to react.

Once we acknowledge to ourselves that there is something going on – right or wrong – we then need to address their concerns without taking their behavior as a personal affront. Most of the time, customers will calm down once they realize they're not helpless.

Start at the Beginning

It never needs to get to the point where the customer becomes abusive. If you buy the idea that difficult customers are not necessarily difficult people, let's treat them like the reasonable people they are. Start at the beginning of the conversation.

I've attended many customer service courses and few of them address the fact that anger can be tempered from the beginning of the conversation. Customer service is not rocket science, but it's definitely more than just being nice. It's acknowledging, right from the start, that the customer is the most important person in the conversation. When the customer knows she's important, the decibel level of her anger goes down significantly.

So, when greeting the customer, do what we said earlier: use your name and use her name. Ask her what you can do for her. Then, let her talk.

Two things can happen. The customer will tell you why she called or came in or she will direct all of her anger from the previous 10 times she called toward you. She will be nice (sometimes annoyed, but nice) or she won't. Let's begin with the upset customer who starts out nice.

After she explains her situation, follow up with a phrase like, "I'll be happy to help you with that."

I know some of you are thinking, "I really don't see myself saying, 'I'll be happy to help you with that.' It sounds so ... so ... fake."

Okay, I'll buy that. If you're not comfortable saying it, don't say it. Instead, use words that make you comfortable:

"I can do that for you."

"I'll be glad to."

"Sure, I can do that."

"Okay, I can help you."

"No problem."

I don't care what you say, as long as it's positive.

Customers have many reasons for coming to you and ask many different questions. But in reality, they all have one unspoken question:

"Are you going to help me?"

The reason this is the one unspoken question is that until you say something in response to their request, complaint, statement or anything else, they don't know if your answer is "yes." By making that positive statement, you are saying "yes." Now the customer knows that he won't have to become upset.

Most of the time, people who serve customers never get to this point – they skip over it all together. Think about the classic way CSRs answer the phone:

"Thank you for calling People to People Learning. My name is Arlene. How may I help you?"

The customer usually responds with a question or problem. Most people react to the customer's situation by either offering solutions or asking questions. But that's exactly what you should *not* do.

Remember, the one unspoken question, regardless of the situation, is "Are you going to help me?" Instead of immediately jumping into solutions or questions, answer the question:

"I can do that for you."

"I can help you with that."

"Let me look into that for you."

"Let's take care of that."

"I'll be delighted to do that for you." (If you like "delighted," by all means, use it! It's a happy word.)

If the problem sounds like it might be one you may not be able to resolve, you can use such answers as:

"Let me see what may be causing the problem."

"I'm not sure what we can do about that, but give me a minute to look into it."

I call it an "invisible hug." When you answer the question, "Are you going to help me" what you're really saying is "Don't you worry about anything. I gotcha! Come here and let me give you a hug." And, as we all know, hugs make everything better.

We can't really hug the customers for it might embarrass them. So we do the next best thing – we tell them we're going to help them.

SHOULD YOU PROBE BEFORE SAYING "I CAN HELP YOU"?

When I talk about this, people often ask, "Isn't it presumptuous to say you can help them when you haven't asked a question to find out if you can? After all, if you say you can help them and then find out you can't, you've not met the customer's expectation." That's a valid point. You may want to ask a question or two before you say you can help. The key here is that you acknowledge their situation before you start asking a bunch of questions.

I have found that if people start asking questions before acknowledging the customer's situation, they rarely come back to the acknowledgement. And the customer never gets that "hug."

YOU'RE ON THEIR SIDE

You've now acknowledged that when customers feel helpless they need to let it out. Since it's not about you, don't take the customer's anger, yelling, screaming, sarcasm, or anything else personally. At this point, customers need to know you are on their side.

They want to know you're there for them and only them.

They want to know they have an advocate.

They want to know you're going to work with them and resolve whatever is wrong.

They want to know you feel their pain.

I know how hard this can be for you. After all, the customer may have just yelled at you or used words you've never used yourself (or at least know you're not supposed to). Worst of all, you know you probably didn't do anything wrong or you know that someone else did the customer wrong.

Whenever a customer has a question to ask or a problem to tell, she has pain. What she's saying to you is "I have pain. I don't want this pain. I want *you* to have my pain instead. Please take my pain from me so that I don't have to feel it anymore!" Customers may not use those exact words (and we can't print the words they sometimes use), but that's what they really mean.

You have to let them know you feel their pain and that you're on their side. If you want the customer to remain calm and to work with you to resolve the situation, the customer must feel that you are attacking the problem as a team. And you need to do so without blaming anybody at your company.

This last action can be a little tricky, though. I worked with a major U.S. city government, teaching their citizen help desk how to deal with citizen problems.

Citizens call 3-1-1 with all kinds of requests and questions like "I need Sanitation to pick up my old refrigerator." In this instance, the operator sends a request to the Sanitation department to pick up the refrigerator and tells the citizen to leave it at the curb on Tuesday night.

On Wednesday, the citizen calls back, complaining that nobody picked up the refrigerator. The operator puts in the request for pick up again and promises the refrigerator will be gone within two days.

The following Wednesday, the citizen calls yet again, informing the operator that "the fridge is still on the street and has been adopted as a new fire hydrant by the neighborhood canines."

By this call, the citizen is livid and begins to raise his voice. A lot. He yells and gets nasty.

Imagine you are the operator. What's the proper response to this customer?

   a) "Yo! Lower your voice. You're hurting my ears!"
   b) "Y'know, I told Sanitation to pick it up twice. So don't take it out on me!"
   c) "Hey! I can't help it if the people in Sanitation are incompetent."
   d) "Let me escalate it to my supervisor for you."
   e) "I agree. That's not acceptable. I'll be glad to look into why it hasn't been picked up yet and take care of it."

The answer, of course, is (e). *It's not rocket service.*

As I said, pushing back against the customer only makes the customer angrier. He doesn't care if his yelling is hurting your ears or if you told Sanitation twice to pick up the refrigerator. All he knows is that he can call 3-1-1 and somebody will pick up his old refrigerator. If Sanitation isn't doing what they are supposed to do, the customer still sees it as *your* fault.

You're right; it's not your fault. But it's also not about you.

EMPATHIZE INSTEAD OF BLAME

When talking to the customer, don't blame anybody. If you blame somebody at the company, you are blaming the whole company. If you blame the company, you are blaming yourself. To the customer, *you* are the company. If you're on his side, then the company is on his side.

So, when a customer calls and starts letting loose, you have to let him know that, at that moment, he is the only customer in the world. When the customer begins to complain, show empathy on three levels: understanding, emotion, and fact/situation. This is a process I learned from Dr. Richard Strand of Customer Focus, Inc. and have seen it used to great effect.

For instance, an empathetic statement would be something like this: "I can see how frustrating it is when Sanitation doesn't pick up your refrigerator."

Let's break this down into the three parts we mentioned earlier:

1. "I can see" shows your understanding.
2. "how frustrating" acknowledges his emotion.
3. "it can be when Sanitation doesn't pick up your refrigerator" restates the facts of the situation.

Think of the response we usually get when we tell our problem to a customer service person. If she wants to help, she might say, "Sorry that happened." For all you know, she may not have heard a word you said! You could have said, "Sanitation didn't pick up my old refrigerator. Since it was still on the street, some kids were playing with it and it fell on one of them, crushing his leg!"

"Sorry that happened."

See what's going on here? It reminds me of when my kids were teenagers. You may have had a similar experience. I would find out one of them did something she wasn't supposed to or didn't do something she was supposed to do. Usually, I was met with this answer:

"sorry."

It's not even a strong "I'm sorry." It's a sheepish, non-connected, impersonal:

"sorry."

I could be criticizing my daughters for not loading their dishes in the dishwasher or I could be screaming because one of them killed the cat. And I would get the same answer:

"sorry."

You don't want to sound like that teenager when you work with customers. You are a person talking to a person. Make it about him. Show him you care. Show him that whatever happened to him is important because it happened to him. Let him know we don't want our customers to feel uncomfortable – ever. We don't ever want our customers to suffer. We don't ever want our customers to feel bad. We don't ever want our customers to be angry – especially at us.

So we make sure *they* know that *we* know what has happened and what they're feeling. Saying "I understand" is great, but it's not enough. You haven't told the customer what you understand or acknowledged how the customer is feeling about it.

When customers are frustrated or annoyed, they want you to know they're frustrated or annoyed. When you acknowledge their emotions, they are more likely to calm down. What a great feeling it is when you are frustrated and someone tells you, with sincerity, "I know how frustrating it can be."

When that happens, the customer thinks, "She understands how frustrating it can be! Wow! She sees I'm frustrated. Wow! It's so great to work with somebody who understands what I'm feeling!" Saying "I know how frustrating it can be" sounds a lot better than "Sorry that happened."

Acknowledge What Happened

Now that we've covered the first two parts of the empathy statement ("I understand how annoying it can be …"), let's move on to the last, and just as important, part of the sentence.

You've shown the customer that you understand ("I can see," "I know," "I acknowledge") and that you feel his emotion (how frustrating, annoying, upsetting, disturbing, aggravating it can be). Now, restate what he told you:

"… when you are left on hold for a half-hour."

"… when you are transferred too many times."

"… when nobody seems to know what he is doing."

"… when they don't pick up your refrigerator."

Let him know you get it. Now, put all three parts together:

- "I understand how frustrating it can be when you are left on hold for a half-hour."
- "I can see how annoying it is when you are transferred too many times."
- "I know how upsetting it is when nobody seems to know what he is doing."
- "I realize how aggravating it can be when they don't pick up your refrigerator."

Wouldn't you feel better if somebody said that to you when you were frustrated instead of just saying "sorry"?

Why is this important? Because the empathy statement says, "I feel your pain." Remember, customers who get upset with you or your company do so because they are angry, frustrated, annoyed, aggravated and feeling helpless. They believe that nobody feels their pain or wants to help them. We turn them around through our actions and our words. Make sure they know you are on their side.

You can put your own spin on the empathy statement, but make sure you touch on all three parts. Let them know you understand, acknowledge their feelings, and repeat what they said so that they know you've heard them.

Do It with Sincerity

You don't have to say the empathy statement in the exact order I just described. You can use the first part, then the third part, and then the second part: "I'm sure seeing the refrigerator on the street every morning can be annoying." Or you could use the third part, then the second part, and then the first part: "Seeing the refrigerator on the street every morning would just put me over the edge! I can see how that would be frustrating!"

Most importantly, what you say needs to be sincere. Say the words with sincerity. Really mean what you say. Sincerity comes when you truly feel the customer's pain because you've seen the same situation happen to other customers, seen a similar situation happen to someone you know really well, or experienced the same situation yourself.

A woman at a health care system I worked with said, "I work with sick and elderly people every day. They come in not feeling like themselves. Often, they're scared and feel helpless. I try to imagine my grandmother or my mother in the same situation. I ask myself how I would treat my mother or my grandmother if she were to come to me with the same pain or problem as this patient. Would I treat her as just another face? Just another disease? No, for me, every patient is my grandmother."

It Really Doesn't Hurt to Apologize

I was talking about apologizing in one of my classes when a participant raised her hand and said, "We've been told that we should never apologize."

At first, I looked at her with disbelief. After a brief period of silence, I managed a suspicious "Why is that?"

"We don't apologize because then we would be accepting blame. And I was told you never accept blame," she continued.

Still in disbelief, I asked again, "Why is that?"

"Because if you accept blame, customers may demand their money back or other compensation. Or they might sue you. It's a legal thing."

"And this policy came from where?"

"I heard it came from the top. The CEO."

It was no wonder this company was in trouble with its customers. The company apparently felt that the customer was the enemy. Even if they did do something wrong, they won't admit it because if they did, the customer might get upset and sue.

That concept is remarkable to me. It's just an excuse for rude behavior. If a customer has the intention to sue, he would probably sue regardless of how you respond. Admitting blame is just one part of it, though. That customer will sue you whether you admit blame or not.

So, how do you stop a customer from suing? It's like the child psychologist said when asked how parents can assure that their children end up being upstanding citizens and all-around good people:

"Well, I can't tell you how to make sure they *will* grow up like that, but I can surely tell you how to make sure they *won't*."

Let me let you in on a little secret: the customer is already angry. The customer is already upset. With a "we never admit we're wrong" policy, you're about to make it worse.

It's not rocket service.

"I Apologize" vs. "I'm Sorry"

One company told me they had no problem with their people apologizing. They just didn't like the words "I'm sorry." They'd rather employees said, "I apologize."

"We like 'I apologize' rather than 'I'm sorry.' 'I'm sorry' sounds like you did something wrong"

"Well, actually, in the customer's mind, you *did* do something wrong. That's why he's upset," I answered.

"Yeah, but I don't want it to sound like I'm admitting it."

Here's the difference between "I apologize" and "I'm sorry": *Apologize* is a verb; it describes an action. When you say, "I apologize," you are saying, "This is what I'm doing." It's an action. You are engaging in the action of apologizing. It doesn't say you feel anything or ensure that you connect with the customer in any way, but it is an apology. I suppose that's okay, but it's not going to make the customer feel like you actually care about her.

Sorry is an adjective. It describes you. *You* are sorry. Being sorry is not an action; it is a feeling, an expression of how you feel. It describes how you feel emotionally. By saying "I'm sorry," you are emotionally connecting with the customer. Since the customer feels helpless, this is what she wants and needs.

Repeat after me:

"I'm sorry."

"I'm sorry."

"I'm sorry."

Did you have trouble with those words rolling off your tongue? Did you feel smaller somehow after saying those words? Those of you who are able to get the words out, either easily or with difficulty, are on the road to better customer relationships. Now say the following:

"I'm really sorry."

"I'm very sorry."

"I'm terribly sorry."

Is this getting easier? Now, say it with sincerity:

"I'm sorry."

"I'm so sorry."

"I'm really sorry."

"I'm very sorry."

"I'm terribly sorry."

Ahhhh. As your customer, I feel better already. Now, follow that with an empathy statement.

"I'm so sorry. I can see how aggravating it can be when nobody wants to take responsibility for a mistake."

You can say "I apologize" or "I'm sorry." They're both good, but "I'm sorry" is better. Unless it will cause you physical pain, say, "I'm sorry." You'll see the difference.

Don't Be Vague

While we're on the subject of apologizing, let me mention one more thing: apologize with all your heart, especially when you're apologizing by email.

Working with a cell phone company's email customer response team, I noticed this statement at the beginning of its standard email response:

"I apologize for *any mistake* we *may have* made."

Hmmm. "I apologize for any mistake we may have made."

Look at how non-committal that statement is. First, the writer uses "I apologize," which we've already discussed, and then follows with "*any* mistake." Any mistake? Do you get the feeling this is a form letter? Does the writer have any idea what the customer's situation really is?

"Any mistake" really says, "Yeah, yeah, yeah, another customer complaining. I don't really care what the problem is, but I'll apologize for ... whatever."

Then we read the last part of this vague statement. So far, the writer has been vague about the apology and vague about what he's apologizing for. To top it off, the writer ends with "we may have caused."

May is one of those hesitant words like might, could, possibly and chance:

"I *might* be able to get that to you tomorrow." (Then again, I might not.)

"I *could* have somebody call you back." (But I won't.)

"It is *possible* that somebody will fix your cable by Tuesday." (But it's not probable.)

"There's a *chance* you could hear from somebody before the end of the day." (There's not a good chance but a chance just the same.)

I've heard people say, "I *might could* do that." That's what I call a *double hesitancy*.

We naturally use hesitant words in our answers to customers and to each other. Many people don't like making commitments. Customers want to know that when you say you're going to help them that they have no reason to believe you won't. They want you to tell them in no uncertain terms what you feel, know, or are able to do. Stay away from vague, hesitant words when talking to a customer in person, on the phone or in email.

If you are hesitant to let customers know you're happy to help them or you're sorry there is a problem, they won't be hesitant to do business with someone else.

React vs. Respond

There are two words in the English language people often perceive to mean the same thing: *react* and *respond*. You hear them used interchangeably all the time but they don't have the same meaning. A reaction is a reflex action. It's almost involuntary or knee-jerk. It's directly from our emotions. A response, on the other hand, is thought out. It's not fast. It's not quick. We take our time. We think about it. We don't let the customer's actions and emotions determine our responses.

In many customer situations, people tend to react more than respond. The customer says something or uses a particularly challenging tone of voice, and then without thinking, we react and say or do something that we shouldn't. They scream and we tell them in no uncertain terms that we will not accept that behavior or worse, we scream back. They become snide and obnoxious and we react accordingly. We don't think about what we do or say; we just react. This is not the way to engender customer loyalty.

One of my customer service class participants listened to me explain this concept, but still looked unconvinced. Noticing her expression, I asked her, "You don't buy this, do you?" She said, "You know, nobody has the right to yell at me. I'm a human being. I have feelings."

I agreed that people shouldn't yell at her, but that doesn't change the fact that people do yell and have no incentive not to. They yell because they are angry and feel helpless. Our job is to make them feel less angry and less helpless. As I explained in the class, "They're not getting paid to be nice. But you are."

After the class participant insisted that the customer had no right to lash out, I asked, "So what do you say when you feel the customer is being abusive?"

"Well, I tell them that I will not be spoken to this way and if they insist on yelling and being abusive, I will just hang up." The whole class wanted to give her a high five and shout, "You go, girl!"

I said, "Let me make sure I understand this. The customer is angry to begin with. He lets it out on you in an effort to show you how angry he is. You tell him you won't take his abuse and that you will hang up if he continues. So tell me, is this action designed to make him *calmer*? Or *angrier*?"

We know it would be so much easier to say, "Oh, yeah? Don't talk to me like that" or be abusive right back to the customer. It might even make us feel better! You can walk away from your desk and announce, "Well I just told an abusive customer who's boss!" and the office staff will carry you on their shoulders in victory.

Actually, that won't happen. Tell the customer you won't take it, and the customer will just get angrier. More than likely, he'll call back and be even more abusive with someone else. Then you'll end up in the doghouse, not only with the customer but also with your co-workers... especially your boss.

What my classroom participant did was *react* to what the customer said when she should have *responded*. Reacting is an action over which we seemingly have no control. We need to respond to the customer's need, not react to the customer's actions. We need to make it about them.

How to Respond

This is where you use all the skills we just talked about. The proper response would be something like this:

"I'm sorry the repairman hasn't shown up. I know how frustrating it can be when you expect somebody to be there and the person doesn't show up. Let me ask you a few questions so I can better help you."

At this point, the customer will probably continue to yell and scream. Let him yell. Let him scream. However, stay calm and say:

"I know how annoying this can be. I'd like to ask you a few questions to clear up the situation. May I ask you a few questions?"

Now that you have again answered him calmly and asked for

permission to get more information from him so that you can help him, he may begin to calm down and cooperate. Or he may continue to yell. Some people say that "three times is the charm" in this situation. So if he continues to yell, it's okay. You just say it again:

"I know how frustrated you are. I really want to help you. May I ask you a few questions to better understand your situation?"

By this time, he should calm down. By your not engaging the customer in the fight, the customer will stop focusing on fighting and instead realize that you are trying to help. Your continuously saying that you want to help will penetrate the anger and help you both focus on solving the situation at hand. But you have to stay calm for this to happen.

When both of you are calm, nobody is out of control. This gives you plenty of room to solve the problem.

You Never Know What Made Them Angry

One of the worst days for a customer is when she realizes she doesn't have a choice. I was able to walk away from the cable TV company, but I couldn't walk away from the health insurance company I wrote about in the last chapter. Like many in the U.S., pre-existing conditions kept my family attached to the company I was with and I had no choice but to let them do what they may. If they wanted to wait until school began to approve my daughter's surgery, I couldn't do anything about it. But like most people in this situation, I did not go quietly. I was not resigned to my fate. I just got angrier and let them know.

I felt helpless.

When an angry customer calls or comes in, we don't know what made him angry. It may indeed have been something to do with your product, service, or company. Or it may be that the problem came on top of five other problems he had that day and the problem with your product just added to the mess. The anger may be a combination of irritation with traffic that morning, frustration with a nasty boss, dissatisfaction with disrespectful kids, or aggravation with his wife's bad mood the night before. He might even be mad at the person who took care of him last time. It could be any number of things. But it is usually not about you.

Angry customers need to vent. Sadly, the venting is often aimed at you, but it's not *about* you. It will only be about you if you fight back and make it about you. Keep your eye on solving the problem and not on the customer's behavior. What matters is solving the problem so that the customer can go on his merry way, happy that somebody finally helped him.

Customers aren't getting paid to be nice. However, you are. I've always wanted to teach a class called "*How to Be a Good Customer*," but nobody wants it. So it's up to you.

It's not rocket service.

Rocket Review

- Difficult customers aren't necessarily difficult people. They just want something done.

- Most people start with good intentions. Very few people wake up in the morning with the intention of making your life miserable.

- Do more responding and less reacting. We are human beings. We have control over our instincts. Have patience.

- Customers want you to "feel their pain." Not only do they want you to feel it, but they also want you to take it away from them. Find a way to do so.

- Show empathy. The customer needs to know that you can put yourself in her shoes and see the world through her eyes.

- Acknowledge what happened. If you acknowledge the customer's situation, you're demonstrating that you aren't taking the company's side against him. Instead, acknowledge what happened and then work on resolving the situation in a way that benefits both the company and the customer.

- Apologize. Say, "I'm sorry." You're not admitting blame. When someone says, "I'm sorry," it changes the whole tone of the conversation.

Manager Lift-Off

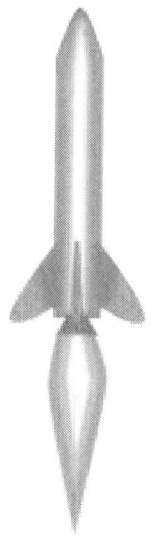

What is the water-cooler conversation in your department? Are your people hanging cartoons with humor based on stupid or demanding customers? Do they roll their eyes when certain customers call? Do your people say things like "This job would be great if it weren't for the customers" when it's actually their job to serve customers?

If so, this should explain why customers aren't happy: the office atmosphere regards the customer as an annoyance. If your people have to deal with a lot of angry or frustrated customers, your job is to give them lots of support. Here are some ideas:

 In team meetings, acknowledge customers can be frustrating, abusive, ignorant, and sometimes out of control. If you can control the conversation, have a discussion on "Our Worst Customers." Let your employees get it all out on the table. Then, work with them to acknowledge that the "worst" customers are rare.

 On the same hand, have a discussion on "Our Best Customers" – customers who made someone happy. This may be a little harder to do, so you may want to offer a prize for the best story.

 Keep making the point that most customers start with good intentions. Model the behaviors of not taking customer complaints personally.

 Let your people know you realize that many of the customers' complaints came because somebody in another department or process caused the problem. Remember, too, that there are things companies can do to fix these situations. But even though someone in your department didn't cause the problem, your department's first responsibility is to the customer.

 Finally, give your employees a space to release their frustrations. Bill Price, the author of *The Best Service is No Service*, tells of a company that actually has a "quiet room" where employees can go to calm down, take a breath or let off steam after a particularly difficult customer or a particularly hard day. Build in time for them to step away. They need it.

COUNTDOWN:

Name that Problem

Many of you may remember an old TV quiz show called *Name that Tune*. The contestants were given a small amount of information about a popular song and then were allowed to hear a few notes of the song to try to figure out the song's name. Contestants competed by wagering their ability to "Name that Tune" in the fewest notes. One contestant would say, "I can name that tune in four notes!" and the other would counter with "I can name that tune in three notes!" The one who was challenged with the fewest notes had to name the tune.

When customer situations come to us, we tend to play a different game called *Name that Problem* or *Name that Solution*. It's a lot like *Name that Tune* but there's no music involved. In this game, the customer starts talking, and as we hear a few words, we think, "I can name that problem or find that solution in two sentences." In other words, we identify a few words or phrases we've heard before and immediately assume the problem is the same as one we've already worked on. So before the customer can finish her explanation, we've already started trying to find the solution. But we may be wrong.

We may be wrong about the problem because we really weren't listening. We were playing *Name that Problem*. And when we try to solve the wrong problem with the wrong solution, we end up making the customer more upset than she was in the first place.

In all fairness, if you're an experienced customer relationship professional, you're good at what you do, which is why it's easy to not listen to what the customer is saying and, more importantly, what the customer is not saying. We hear dozens, if not hundreds, of problems each week. We know the traits and characteristics of particular situations, so we're quick to solve the problem based on those traits and characteristics we're familiar with. The worst thing that can happen, though, is we assume that what the customer is telling us is what is actually going on.

Do customers always know what they're talking about? If you deal with customers, you know the answer is "no." Customers only know what they know. They will tell you what they know and what they think the problem is because they don't want to look stupid. And the more technical your position, the more likely it is they don't want you to think they're stupid. People are very insecure about their technical understanding or lack thereof.

Then there are customers who will feign ignorance on technical problems so the support person will speak slower with less technical jargon. In any case, our job is to make sure we understand the situation. And the best way to make sure we understand the situation is to ask questions. Don't accept the customer's potentially misguided interpretation of her problem without making sure it's the correct problem. Yet don't make customers feel stupid by telling them their assessment is wrong.

You're diagnosing just like a doctor. How do you feel when a doctor lets you off with a diagnosis before you told him all your symptoms?

QUESTIONS ARE THE GREAT DIFFUSERS OF ANGRY SITUATIONS

Even if you play *Name that Problem* and you can guess the problem in three words, don't guess. In fact, don't guess – even if you're sure or even if you're absolutely positive! Instead, ask as many questions as you possibly can without overdoing it.

Ask questions to clarify something the customer said, to give you more information, or to confirm what you've already figured out. Ask questions, especially if the customer is upset and angry. Ask questions even though you know the customer wants a solution NOW! Ask questions so the customer knows you are paying attention.

Remember that statement we say when a customer seems to be out of control?

"I know how annoying this can be. I'd like to ask you a few questions to clear up the situation. May I ask you a few questions?"

Questions are the great diffusers of angry situations. They make the customer feel valued, listened to, and the center of attention. As long as you're asking the customer to explain the situation from his point of view, tell you what he thinks needs to be done, and/or to tell you the consequences of his situation, the customer will not get any angrier and may in fact become less angry. Then the focus is on the customer and his situation, not on you or the company. Remember, it's about the customer. The customer is the most important person in the conversation.

CUSTOMERS LIKE BEING THE CENTER OF ATTENTION

In Countdown Chapter 8, I told the story about the woman who showed me her pay stub which said, "This paycheck is brought to you by your customers." When your customers provide your paycheck, they become entitled to certain things. One of those things is your attention.

The conversation between you and the customer is about her. When she calls you on the phone, comes into the store or restaurant, engages you in a chat, or interacts with you in any way, she wants to be the center of attention and the center of the conversation. If she wants to give you information, it needs to be her information about what's important to her. If you need to give her information, it needs to relate to her problem, her desire, or her pain.

The best way to make her the center of attention is to ask questions. There is no reason to talk about you or your needs when solving *her* problem. She doesn't care about what you want, what you need, or your desires. She will care about what you *think*, but only after you've asked her enough questions.

ASK THE CUSTOMER QUESTIONS …

Imagine you're talking to a help desk representative and you are calling about your DSL service:

"My DSL is on the blink. When I stream video, it stops, starts, jumps, and dies."

"Oh really?" she responds. "That's too bad. Have I told you about our new, upgraded DSL service for only $7.50 more per month?"

Did her response make you feel like she had your best interests in mind? Who was her response about? You or her?

Well, of course it was about her. She didn't care a whit about what you wanted, what you needed, what you felt, what your problem was, or what she could do to help you. She just wanted to upgrade your service at a higher price and maybe get a commission. You were upset and helpless and she didn't care.

Customers need you to show them you're paying attention. Instead of first offering the upgraded DSL service, the DSL help desk person should have asked you a few questions. The answers would have indicated a simple problem that did not require a major solution. At the very least, she could have gathered some information that would have helped her determine whether you were calm, upset, angry, or looking for an upgrade. You may have actually needed to upgrade your service, but for her to know, she needs to ask questions.

When you ask customers questions about their wants, needs, and situation, they get the idea you are interested in them. They feel as though you are focusing all of your attention on them and only them. They feel like the most important people in the conversation. They feel like you care about them. They feel like people being served by people. They feel like they're talking to a fellow human being, not a company employee.

... But Don't *Attack* the Customer with Questions

Still, it's not so simple to ask questions. Customers can perceive your questions as an attack. You're asking them to do something they weren't intending to do: you asked them a question and now they're obligated to answer. They may not want to answer. They may not know the answer. They may not trust you yet. They may not feel you have their best interests in mind.

When I was a news reporter many years ago, I used to interview politicians. Politicians are taught how to avoid answering reporters' questions. They are also instructed to ensure the focus stays on what *they* want to say. In other words, they don't let reporters lead them.

Knowing this, I would try to make politicians as uncomfortable as possible so they would tell me what I wanted to know, not just what they wanted to say. I would ask them question after question, often in a rapid-fire process. I realized that if they didn't know what question was coming next then they wouldn't have time to think in advance about how to answer it.

However, when *you* ask *your* customer questions, you want to do the complete opposite. You want him to be as *comfortable* as possible. You want him to feel you care about him and his situation, not like you are interrogating him. You want to lead into your questions.

Leading into questions means prefacing your question with a statement to inform the customer what's coming next. As I mentioned earlier, people have a basic human need to know what's coming. It gives us a feeling of control. We like control.

So before asking a question, say something like "Let me ask you a question" or "May I ask you a question about..." Sometimes you can say, "You said you were having trouble with the unit, so let me ask you a question about that. What exactly is happening when you turn it on?"

Notice what just happened:

First, I mentioned what the customer said, which does two things: I acknowledge there is a problem or situation that is important to him and then I tell him exactly what I will be asking.

Second, I asked for permission to ask a question about what he already mentioned. Customers like to be the ones giving permission. It gives them control.

Third, I asked a wide-open question, allowing him to give me as much information as I need to solve his problem. But the most important thing I did was give him a sense of control over the situation as well as my role in addressing his needs. By doing so, I made the conversation about him, not me.

The customer's brain processes the words in split seconds, telling itself, "Oh, he heard what I said and now he wants to ask me a question about ... what? Oh, what I already told him! Good, I know all about that subject! Now he just asked me the question he told me he was going to ask me. I'm ready!"

No attack.

No interrogation.

No fear.

No discomfort.

No abusive customer.

No conflict.

And lots of customer control.

When customers feel like they are in control, they are less likely to become angry, abusive or out of control. They are less likely to escalate or give up. They are less likely to spread the word about what they perceive as your incompetence. You may not be incompetent at all, but perception is reality to your customers.

OPEN AND CLOSED QUESTIONS

Once you start asking questions, you have to know how to ask the *right* kinds of questions. If you ask the wrong kinds of questions, you'll get the wrong kinds of answers.

Questions fall into two categories: open and closed. An open question asks, "How did the accident happen?" or "What may I help you with today?" or "What's goin' on?" The customer can give you any number of different answers to an open question. She will more likely expand on the answer. Sometimes, an open question will trigger a long rant, and that's okay because at least the customer is providing you with information.

A closed question asks, "Did you turn on the computer before you called me?" or "What color did you expect to get?" or "Herr Wagner, do you spell your name with a V?" With these questions, you are asking the customer for a specific answer, frequently yes or no. Details are not allowed. If you want details, ask an open question.

We ask open questions when we need to gather information and closed questions when we have some idea of what the problem is and want to confirm our theory. If the answer to your closed question is no, don't take it personally. It's just time to ask another open question to gather more information.

THE NON-QUESTION QUESTION

Sometimes, the best way to ask an open question is not to ask a question at all. It's what I call the non-question question. Just shut up and the customer will tell you everything you need to know.

When I was a radio talk show host, I would interview many of the political and business "celebrities" in my area. In an effort to make the show a conversation and not just a series of questions, the conversation would occasionally go like this:

Me: "Senator, there are many people who would say this bill has no chance of passing ... ever."

Senator: (silence)

Me: (silence)

Senator: (after a little more silence) "Well, Steve, the opponents of this bill just don't care about the children of our county."

The next day, the headlines read **"Senator: Bill opponents don't care about kids."**

Sometimes, making a statement and waiting for a reply is as good as or even better than asking an open question. People say, "Nature abhors a vacuum." If you make a statement and leave it hanging, somebody will make the next statement. Since *you're* not going to fill the silence, the other person in the conversation will. By reacting to the silence, he will tell you more than he ever would have in responding to a question – without even realizing it.

Great salespeople know this to be true. The best salespeople never sabotage their sale by talking. They stop talking and let the customer make the decision. You can do the same thing. Give customers the opportunity to give you the information you need or to solve their own problem.

Just a note: for some people, the silence we talked about earlier may make them uncomfortable, nervous and they may also think you're weird. So silence should be used judiciously.

You can also ask a non-question question by starting the statement with "Tell me more" or "Fill me in."

"Tell me more about what happened." "Fill me in on what took place."

Neither of these statements end with a question mark. However, they're definitely questions. "Tell me more" and "Fill me in" are also great ways to begin follow-up questions.

Mixing non-question questions with regular open questions makes the questioning process more conversational and, therefore, more comfortable for the person answering the questions.

Confirm Your Understanding

After you've led into your questions and have asked all kinds of open questions to gather information, you should have a pretty good idea of what the problem or situation is. At this point in the conversation, it's perfectly acceptable to play *Name that Problem*. After all, you're not jumping to any conclusions or relying on your recollections of previous customers' situations. You're using the information you gathered from *this* customer and whether it's something you've heard before or not, you have connected with this customer's uniqueness.

This is where you begin to ask closed questions to get that final piece of information and confirm that you have the right answers.

"Did the washing machine begin making that noise *after* the water started coming in?"

"Does the DSL light blink, stay dark, or just light up when you turn the computer back on?"

You can ask closed questions to confirm by using what I call the "echo technique" and repeating or paraphrasing what the customer already said:

"So the computer refuses to reboot every time you load a new piece of software." Or "So the computer refuses to reboot every time you load the Microsoft security updates but not when you load any other software. Is that correct?"

When you ask closed questions to confirm what you heard, you give the customer a chance to correct your perception or to agree that what he said was correct. As stated earlier, customers don't always know what the problem is, and even if they do, they don't always explain things well. This is especially true when they are angry or upset. Think about the last time you were angry or upset. Do you think there was a good chance you said things you shouldn't have and didn't provide information you should have? None of us are at our best when we're upset.

When you use the "echo technique" and you repeat back (or paraphrase) what they've said, you confirm that you've heard everything, that you're both on the same page and that you were listening and paying attention – to them.

THE ECHO TECHNIQUE CAN BE ANNOYING

Often, people will argue that the echo technique can be annoying. Repeating everything the customer has just said can cause somebody to lash out and say, "Yeah, that's what I said. Didn't you hear me the first time?" or even "What are you, deaf?" (A class participant in Brooklyn, NY mentioned that one.)

I can see why customers would say things like that. After all, they just took the time to tell you all the information you asked about. Now you're asking them if they said what they said.

Instead of just plunging in with the repetitive echo, say something like, "I want to make sure I heard everything that you said" or "I'm going to repeat back what I believe I heard you say. Please let me know if I heard wrong."

Always put the onus on you. Never say, "I want to make sure you explained it well." When it comes to communication, it's never the customer's fault. It's always because you didn't understand, you didn't hear, you didn't comprehend, or you didn't get it. Accusing her of not explaining it right or communicating it well will only worsen the situation.

The customer's expectation was that she would explain everything and that you would hear and understand everything. When you repeat what she said without prefacing your remarks, you don't meet her expectation. So, you preface the echo with a statement like the ones I just mentioned and reset her expectation. If the expectation is wrong or if the situation changes, we have to reset the expectation.

USING THE ECHO TECHNIQUE EFFECTIVELY

I've heard a story from several different speakers that breaks me up each time I hear it. The details are not always the same, but the story still makes a great point.

A man comes home from a business trip. His wife picks him up at the airport. After he gets in the car he asks, "How was your day?"

"How was my day? How was my day? I had a terrible day!" she replies.

"You had a terrible day?" he counters.

"Yes, I had a terrible day. My boss was on the rampage!"

"Your boss was on the rampage?" he answers, his eyes wide.

"Yes! He took off after Debbie ..."

"He took off after Debbie?"

"Yeah! And he used words ... you know the words he uses ..." she says in disgust, getting angrier and angrier.

"I know the words he uses!" he replies.

"Well, I tell you, if he ever uses those words with me, I'm not going to take it!"

"If I were you, I wouldn't take it!"

"I WON'T!"

The conversation continued that way for another 20 minutes until they arrived home, during which he would continue to repeat only the last few words of every sentence she said.

That night when they went to bed, she hugged him, saying, "Thank you for listening before. Darling, you are the most wonderful husband any woman could ever have."

The echo technique works. In this case, it showed empathy, which is all she needed.

DON'T BE SO QUICK TO SAY "NO!"

We now know the customer doesn't always know what she is talking about. Our job is to make sure we don't make her look stupid. Customers hate looking stupid.

Often when customers talk to us, they are in a state of increased agitation. They're upset and they want satisfaction. Then when they scream, we react rather than respond. We try to solve their problem, even though it may not be the problem that needs solving. And if we find that we cannot do what the customer wants, we say the word guaranteed to increase the already increased agitation further: NO!

Even when we think the answer is no, we first need to make sure that "no" is the only answer we can give. Even though we may not be able to do what they want us to do, customers will often be satisfied with a different solution. However, we can't find another solution unless we ask questions.

For instance, I was working with the employees of an institution of higher learning. In the class were people who worked in virtually every department at the college: registrar, bursar, counseling, guidance, writing center, library, financial aid, office of the dean of students, etc. I asked if there were times when they have to say no to a student. An employee from the financial aid office raised her hand.

"When do you have to say no?" I asked.

"When a student has used all of the financial aid available to him from the school and wants more," she answered.

I then clarified from the employee that the student had taken out student loans and received some minor scholarships but that he still had a good amount to pay on his tuition and fees. Then I asked a non-question question, "So, by taking out all of those loans and receiving those scholarships, he had exhausted what the college could do for him."

"Correct," she said, with all the certainty of a woman who had been asked if the sky was blue on a clear day.

"What does the student want?" I asked.

The class participants looked at me puzzled. I heard the words "more financial aid" from several people, but it was muted. So I asked again, "What does the student want?"

A brave soul called out, "More financial aid!" "Yes!" I shouted back. "And we can't give it to him, correct?" The class nodded their heads in agreement. So I asked, "How can we help him get more financial aid?" They looked at me like I had four heads. I repeated the question.

A woman in the back of the room finally spoke up and said, sheepishly, "By telling him about other scholarships and aid that may be available to him from other sources." Yes, the school was not the only source of aid. A whole community out there could possibly provide financial assistance.

"So what question or questions could we ask him to help him go that route?"

They quickly volunteered such questions as "Have you considered looking in other places for scholarship money?" and "Do your parents belong to a union from which you may be able to get a scholarship?" and "What service organizations do you or your parents belong to?" and so on. It was amazing the amount of questions and possibilities that broke loose when they pulled away from the idea that the only thing they could do for this student was provide assistance directly from the college or traditional government loan sources.

It doesn't matter how important or small the request is. If you think you have to say "no," seek out ways to avoid doing so and find alternatives to what the customer requested. When I was working with a hospital, an employee said that patients call all the time saying, "I need to see the doctor NOW!" even though the doctor had no more appointments available that day. After questioning one particular patient, it turned out that she felt lousy and wanted a doctor to see her *as soon as possible*. The participant's solution was to tell the patient that she could come to the doctor's office and wait to see if another patient didn't show up or if the doctor finished early with a patient.

The key here was asking questions to find out what the situation was and how soon the patient *really* needed to see the doctor. If the patient insisted on seeing the doctor that day, the solution above seemed to be the best the doctor's office could do without putting off the patient until the next day.

However, I challenged the employees once more.

"Is there anything else you can do to help the patient avoid having to wait until tomorrow to be treated for her illness?"

After much thought, one participant called out, "We could send her to the local free-standing emergency room." Another quickly jumped in and added, "And we could call the emergency room to let them know she was coming so they'd be ready for her."

Bingo!

Sometimes You Have to Say No

I'm not saying you should never say no to a customer. There are times when no is the only answer. In those cases, we let the chips fall where they may and we'll touch on how to handle that when we count down to Chapter 3. However, if this process reduces the number of times you have to say no by even 25%, you will have fewer angry or upset customers.

Customers have good intentions most of the time. They just want to get something done. They have a problem, they want you to solve it, and if you do, they're happy. Some customers can stomp around, especially when you tell them "no." So if they can't have what they want, perhaps they'll settle for something else. In any case, the more you can do to find a way to make the customer the least bit happy, the better the customer will feel about you and your company, and the happier and calmer you will both be.

It's not rocket service.

ROCKET REVIEW

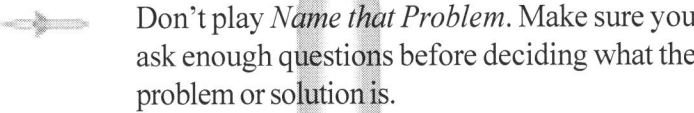

- Don't play *Name that Problem*. Make sure you ask enough questions before deciding what the problem or solution is.

- Questions are great diffusers of difficult situations because they show the customer you are paying attention.

- Questions can be perceived as an attack. Make sure that you lead into your questions to let the customer know that you're going to ask something.

- Open questions help you gather information; closed questions help you confirm you are on the right track.

- Don't be so quick to say "no." Just like playing *Name that Problem*, ask questions to find out if there may be an alternative solution to make the customer happy.

MANAGER LIFT-OFF

Many managers do more telling than asking. They fall into a habit of exerting control by instructing, setting the pace, and making the plans that everybody must follow. They believe that since they set up the plan, they must know the best way to implement the plan. If you continually do this, you'll begin to wonder why your staff has a distinct lack of initiative.

I had a boss once who held meetings to describe a new initiative, process, or way of doing things. After revealing this information, he'd ask the group for feedback. This happened at every meeting. At his early meetings, staff members would happily volunteer their thoughts, after which the boss would proceed to let them know why their idea was good or bad – mostly bad. After a while, they stopped giving ideas and the only ones who responded were the new hires who didn't know any better.

When the boss asked for feedback, the employees believed he really wanted their opinions and ideas. When he continually rejected those opinions and ideas, they began to wonder why he was asking. Worst of all, they ended up believing he didn't want their opinions at all and he didn't trust them – which is what the boss was communicating.

Just like external customers, your employees want to feel they're the center of attention. They want to know that *you* want to know what they think. The more you ask their opinions and thoughts and take action on them, the more loyal they'll be to you and the less they'll bitch and moan at the water cooler. They'll believe they are valued contributors to the direction and productivity of the group. More than likely, they'll stay longer because if the group is working on their own idea (or an idea on which they had input) they will want to stick around to see it through. So, here are some things you can do:

→ When revealing new initiatives or ideas, ask your people how they believe it can be implemented best before you tell them your ideas. The staff will appreciate your interest in their ideas.

→ Every 4-6 months, hold an "only the staff talks" meeting. The staff offers ideas on how to make the department more productive, how to implement ideas, how to raise morale, etc. You, as the manager, are only allowed to ask questions. You may not comment on the ideas and you may only use open questions unless you are clarifying. Just make sure, though, that your clarifying statements aren't judgmental, for example, "So, you don't think your idea is stupid, right?" Be careful: if you ask for ideas, you'd better implement some of them and explain why you're not implementing others.

→ When reviewing an employee's work or behavior, always ask open questions that tell the employee you're interested in her take on the situation before you give your opinion. Acknowledge what she tells you, then say what you think.

→ Create a policy that says, "50% of the processes we have instituted in this department come from our employees' ideas." When employees see that you are interested in their ideas and then see that you are committed to using them, employee engagement will soar.

COUNTDOWN:

Be a Customer Advocate

Customer experience guru Lior Arussy, CEO of the Strativity Group, loves to tell the story of the corporate lawyer who says he has nothing to do with the company's customers. Not knowing at first that he was a company attorney, Lior asked, "You don't touch the customer at all? Which department are you in?"

"I'm in legal," the lawyer replied.

"You're in legal. I see. What do you do in legal?" Lior continued.

"I protect the company," he proudly answered.

"Who do you protect the company from?" Lior asked.

"The customers!" exclaimed the lawyer.

It's pretty amazing when you think about it. Most major companies, and quite a few minor ones, have a department whose sole purpose is to protect the company from the people most responsible for its success. Now, I understand that customers sue companies and that in order to battle these suits they need a legal department. But it seems perverse that there are people working for a company who see the customer as the enemy.

The customers, as I mentioned earlier, are not the enemy. They are our best friends. They buy our products. They buy our services. They pay their bills. In turn, they pay *our* bills because we make money when they do all of these things. We like these people.

Therefore, we need to be customer advocates. Instead of protecting the company from our customers, we need to be creating an environment where not only are they our best friends but we are their best friends, too. We want them to like us as much as we like them.

So what does it mean to be a customer advocate?

Customer advocates put the customer first. As I said before, the customer is the most important person in the conversation. This is the opposite of what most corporate cultures teach. Most of the time, quite a lot of lip service is paid to the idea that the customer is most important, but we all know that the "customer-centric" organizational chart and the real organizational chart have little in common.

Some of you may have seen the "customer-centric" organizational chart. It features a typical organizational breakdown, but with the company at the bottom, management just above the company, company employees (especially customer-facing employees) above management, and all the way at the top – at the center of attention – is The Customer. This organizational structure makes everybody feel good, especially the people who came up with the chart. The message: "The customer is at the center of everything we do. Nothing – Nothing – Nothing is more important than the customer."

Of course, when a customer is frantic because the materials haven't arrived and you are not responsible, some things can seem to be more important than the customer:

"I'm sorry, but the person who handles that isn't here. She won't be in until the morning. I'll have her call you as soon as she gets in."

Who was the most important person in this conversation? Not the customer. Will the customer have to wait because it's not your job? If I'm the customer, I need those materials by the morning and having my account manager call me in the morning isn't going to do me any good. Nothing – Nothing – Nothing is more important than my getting those materials by the morning.

It's time to figure out how to be a customer advocate.

I had a customer advocate situation with a supervisor named Dan Nelson at an AT&T call center. I was so moved by his advocating on my behalf that I wrote a blog post about him:

CUSTOMER SERVICE HERO: DAN NELSON, AT&T

Early yesterday afternoon, this was going to be a blog post trashing my DSL provider, AT&T, not because something went wrong, but because when it did go wrong, nobody seemed to be able to help me ... until Dan Nelson.

Dan Nelson is a customer service supervisor in AT&T's DSL call center. He is also this blog's first Customer Service Hero.

We had three phone lines with AT&T: one line for the home (8329), one line for the business (3042) and one for the fax and DSL service (3142). Since we rarely receive faxes anymore, we decided to eliminate the 3142 line and receive faxes on one of our other two lines. However, in order to cancel the 3142 line, we needed to move our DSL service to the 3042 line. My wife and business partner, Arlene, called AT&T Wednesday morning to do just that.

One of AT&T's DSL customer service representatives served her and arranged to 1) move the DSL to the 3042 line and then 2) close down the 3142 line. Arlene was told that the transfer would take place on June 4 (a week later) and that the DSL service would remain on 3142 in the meantime. The CSR reiterated several times that the 3142 line would not be disconnected before the DSL was transferred.

Thursday morning, we went down to our office and went online without trouble, and then, at around 9:00 a.m., the Internet went out. After trying a few things, Arlene contacted AT&T and found out – you guessed it – the internet was out because they had shut down the 3142 line before transferring the DSL. For almost an hour, the CSR attempted to find out what she could do, only for us to learn that we were out of luck. We would have to wait until June 4 for the transfer to take place. No internet for a week. We said that was unacceptable and pushed her to expedite the transfer. She said Arlene would need to call back in a couple of hours, when another CSR would call the department responsible to find out what could be done. When Arlene called back, she was told that her request had been rejected and that we would still need to wait until June 4. This is when she handed the phone to me and when I first talked with Dan Nelson.

Dan immediately showed empathy for our situation and explained to me that it was the dispatch area denying my request. I told him that I teach customer service and that one of the first tenets of good customer service is the motto "If you break it, you fix it." As I said, "This was not my fault or Arlene's fault. It was AT&T's fault. When you screw up, everything else is superseded to fix the problem for the customer." Dan then did what I teach: He took my problem, owned it and did not let go until it was solved.

First, he contacted the dispatch people to move things along but they stonewalled him. They said they might be able to reinstate our DSL service on June 3. Dan called me back and told me what the dispatch people had said, but before I could get upset, he informed me that he was going to try instead to contact the accidental disconnect department to get the 3142 line reactivated. However, they told him that they couldn't reactivate 3142 because I already had an open order for a transfer to the 3042 line!

Dan then told me that he had two people at higher levels who he thought might be able to help break through the red tape. But he couldn't call them; he had to email them and probably wouldn't get a response for a few hours. (Nobody can contact anybody by phone? This is AT&T – the phone company!) I told him I would wait. He had already won my confidence.

Shortly before 5 p.m., Dan called back and said that our transfer would take place before end of day Friday, which was the next day, and he would call us to make sure it had occurred. Around 2:45 Friday afternoon, Dan called, walked me through the setup process and didn't get off the phone until my DSL service was back up and running.

Dan Nelson made my problem his problem. While the CSRs were very nice, nice was not enough when the other departments didn't seem to care about my situation. Dan cared, did what he had to in order to resolve my situation, and didn't let go of my problem until I was happy. For that, Dan Nelson, AT&T customer service supervisor, is a Customer Service Hero.

(By the way, my blog is www.SteveCohn.ItsNotRocketService.com)

It is true that Dan Nelson was a supervisor and probably had more leeway to do what he did than did the hundreds of representatives at AT&T's call centers. I don't know how much flexibility the people who worked under him had to make the same kinds of decisions. My feeling is Dan was able to do what they couldn't.

But that doesn't mean they shouldn't be able to make those decisions. I may be talking in a world that doesn't exist in your situation. Okay, fine. That doesn't change what customers expect and what they judge you on when deciding to continue to do business with you and recommend you to others.

The customer needs an advocate. The customer needs to know that when he calls, emails, or comes to the counter that somebody will take care of his situation. It means that even if you can't help him, you will find somebody who will. It means that when you see the same issues repeatedly occurring, you will inform somebody who has the power to do something about it.

While we shouldn't be customer advocates at the expense of hurting the company, being a customer advocate also means that there are times when we shouldn't protect the company at the expense of creating an unhappy customer. One employee at a company I worked with shared that he was instructed to "make something up" so that a customer wouldn't find out that her sales representative had been fired days before and hadn't been replaced. So the employee returned the customer's call and said the sales rep was out sick and would call the customer when he got back. The customer then asked the obvious question – "When will he be back?" Instead of saying "I don't know" he said, "I believe he'll be back on Wednesday."

Guess what's going to happen on Wednesday?

Being a customer advocate means trusting customers with the truth.

TRUST CUSTOMERS TO HANDLE THE TRUTH

Explaining bad news to an angry and upset customer is a defining moment as a customer advocate. Companies and service providers have a number of these defining moments during each customer interaction, from how they show empathy and ask questions to how they solve the customers' problems. But one of the most important defining moments is how you handle explaining bad news.

Employees and companies often have no problem being customer advocates until something goes wrong. Then, they have to tell the customer the bad news – like the sales rep has been fired. Since the employee now has to explain that something has changed or something went wrong, she becomes like the guy in legal – "protect, protect, protect!" And customer advocacy goes out the window. In actuality, the window is closed altogether. Sadly, our first inclination in protecting is to shade the truth, to make something up, stall, or lie.

The first step in explaining bad news is to tell the truth. That's right. Trust customers to handle the truth because they can. And let me tell you, they will be angrier if they find out you lied to them than if you tell them the truth, even if it's something they don't like or necessarily want to hear.

You don't have to give them every detail, blame anybody, or criticize the company or another employee. But, as the saying goes, the truth will set you free.

In a retail sales seminar, I told the group that they should tell the truth all the time. One person asked, "So, if there's going to be a 25-minute wait, should I tell them?"

"Well, what would you say instead?"

"Say what I always do – 'It'll be a few minutes.'"

Have you ever been in this situation? A salesperson says, "It'll be a few minutes" but then it turns out to be 25 minutes before he gets to you. How angry are you with each five minutes that passes? Wouldn't it be better if the salesperson told you originally, "It will be 25 minutes"?

The seminar participant challenged me: "But if telling the customers the truth makes them leave and go somewhere else, I'll lose those sales!"

Here's the way I figure it: If someone tells me it's going to be 25 minutes before anyone will help me, I have options. She has set my expectations. I can wait, knowing it will be 25 minutes, and not get angry when it actually takes 25 minutes; I can come back later, when it might be less busy; I can ask the salesperson when it would be better for me to come back; or I can shop at another store.

If the customer has to wait far longer than he expects, you're not getting the sale anyway! If you lie to the customer, he's never coming back. At least if you tell the truth, he might buy something from you at a later time.

UNDERPROMISING AND OVERDELIVERING

While we're on the subject of telling customers the truth, I'd like to address something that is always said when teaching about serving customers: under-promise and over-deliver.

I hear it all the time: "Under-promise and over-deliver. Promise your customer a little less and then deliver a little more." In other words, if you know it's going to take two days for a shipment to arrive, tell the customer it will take four days, so when it arrives in two days the customer is thrilled. You look great because you exceeded his expectations. It's an easy way to make the customer happy.

In many cases, it's also lying, especially when it comes to time estimates.

We're not talking about hedging your bets. If you know something should take three hours to finish, but you know there's a decent possibility it could take five hours, tell the customer you'll have it to her in five hours. This way, you're not lying. Even though there's an 85% chance it will take only three hours, you're not boxing yourself into a corner by committing to something that might not happen. That's okay and understandable.

What we're talking about is not doing this just to make yourself look good. Don't pad the estimate even though you know there's no way it will ever take as long as you promise. Customers catch on to these things, and worse than that, the customer might actually become angry. I was discussing this when working with an electric utility. One of the class participants noted that if he tells a supermarket owner that his electricity will be back on in six hours during a power outage, the supermarket owner is going to send most of his staff home and likely close the store. If the power comes back on in an hour or two, the supermarket owner is going to be annoyed.

Others have said, "But what if it has nothing to do with time? What if I promise the customer that my service includes certain activities, but when I deliver the service, I do even more?"

That's okay. Adding more to the service or throwing in a few extras is under the vendor's control. If the customer is happy in accepting what you promised, she'll be even happier if you give more.

Always remember, though, customers change their expectations. Years ago, I used to belong to a CD club, ordering music through the mail. Whenever I sent in my order, the order form would say, "Allow 3-4 weeks for delivery." The CDs would most often come within two weeks. Then, my ordering method changed. I started ordering online. Using the online system, the CD club could process my order faster. I began to receive my order within a week to 10 days after I ordered. Yet the online order form still said, "Allow 3-4 weeks for delivery."

One time, my kids decided to order some CDs for me for Father's Day. They ordered the CDs a couple of weeks before the holiday. Soon, Father's Day came and went and I hadn't received the CDs. I called the CD club and they noted that it had only been two-and-a-half weeks since the order and they said, "Allow 3-4 weeks for delivery." I said, "That's true, but I usually get my order within a week to ten days." They said, "Well, on Father's Day, Christmas, Mother's Day, and Valentine's Day, that's not the case."

My expectations had changed because they so consistently over-delivered that it became normal to me. When their stated promise of three-to-four weeks came true at Father's Day, I wasn't happy.

INSTITUTIONALIZED LYING

I was working with a software company – a very, very large software company with three initials – and when I asked "What gets in the way?" they told me that their salespeople will promise a customer that the software or hardware can do something it can't. The salespeople know they're lying to the customer, but they do it anyway. Perhaps I was naïve, but I said, "Why would they do that? Why would the salesperson lie and say the software can do something it can't?" (Silly me!)

"Because then they wouldn't get the sale," one class participant replied.

"Is it that your software can't do what the customer wants it to do but your competitor's software can?" I asked.

"No, the competitor's software doesn't do it, either," another participant piped in. "But they tell the customer that it can, so our salespeople have to also. In the end, we have to clean up for their shading the truth."

"So just because they lie, we have to lie too?" I said, totally non-plussed. "Why don't we create a competitive advantage by positioning ourselves as 'the honest company'? In other words, 'They'll lie to you, but we won't.'"

The class looked at me with facial expressions that said, "*You* know that, and *we* know that, but that's the way the system works." One company lies, so the other company lies and before long, such lying becomes institutionalized. Some major changes in thinking have to happen to fix this.

Think about how many people this institutionalized lying affects. The customer service people or the help desk gets hurt because they receive the wrath of the customer when the software doesn't perform as promised. The customer gets hurt because she bought a bill of goods that doesn't exist. The sales representative hurts himself because the customer won't buy from him again, and the company itself gets hurt because the customer raises her expectations and the company can't deliver. Even if the competition does it too, the company suffers, because when the customer knows everybody lies, she has no loyalty and will buy only on price – until she finds a company that will be honest with her.

Trust customers to handle the truth. The customer may still not like the situation, but at least you have his trust. And trust is an important step in being a customer advocate and keeping the relationship with the customer.

It's not rocket service.

DON'T MAKE THE CUSTOMER DO UNNECESSARY WORK

This is a fascinating story from the Associated Press:

"A New Hampshire man says he swiped his debit card at a gas station to buy a pack of cigarettes and was charged over 23 quadrillion dollars. Josh Muszynski checked his account online a few hours later and saw the 17-digit number – a stunning $23,148,855,308,184,500 (twenty-three quadrillion, one hundred forty-eight trillion, eight hundred fifty-five billion, three hundred eight million, one hundred eighty-four thousand, five hundred dollars)."

This story has been all over the Web. Most people have talked about the bank's incredible mistake – "Can you believe it? 23 quadrillion dollars?" The mistake is almost too silly to make a big deal over.

Or is it? In reading the story, the ridiculously large number isn't what caught my eye. It was this passage:

"Muszynski says he spent *two hours* on the phone with Bank of America trying to sort out the string of numbers and the $15 overdraft fee."

TWO HOURS? What could have been happening on that call for two hours? Did the representative(s) have to follow every procedure in order to figure out that he didn't spend that kind of money? And even if they did, why did the customer need to stay on the phone while they did so? In a TV interview, Muszynski said the CSR didn't quite know what to do with his situation.

This is a customer advocacy moment of truth.

Here's what should have happened: Muszynski sees the number on his statement. After going back to the gas station, he calls Bank of America. A representative answers the phone and says, "How may I help you today?" Muszynski says, "There's a charge on my debit card for $23,148,855,308,184,500." The rep says, "Hmm ... Let me call up your account ... I have it here, Mr. Muszynski. Oh, wow! I do see that number. That is clearly a mistake. Let me check into it and remove it from your account. I'll call you when it's done. What is the best number to reach you?"

And that would be that. No two hours on the phone, no holding for help, no confused representatives making him wait. I timed this imaginary interaction. It took exactly one minute, not two hours.

The situation should have been handled this way because the mistake was so obvious and so ridiculous that anybody could see that it was a mistake, and not Muszynski's mistake.

It's not rocket service.

There are two people involved in this stage of the story – Muszynski and the service representative. The service rep is supposed to be the customer's advocate. So when the rep saw the number on the statement on her screen, she should have ended Mr. Muszynski's involvement in this issue. It's not his job to wait while everybody figures it out.

There was no way the bank was not going to remove the charge or blame him for charging that much. (Muszynski said in the interview that he thought his identity was compromised and that somebody must have used his card to buy Europe.) The customer should not have had to wait while the bank figured out what happened, how it happened, and whose fault it was. (It turned out to be Visa's fault – 13,000 other customers had the same mistake.) So why did it take so long?

You Don't Have to Hurt the Company

If you recall, I said earlier that the customer is not always right. There is no contradiction between that and being a customer advocate. There is no contradiction between being a customer advocate and protecting the company's interests. There is no contradiction between being a customer advocate and protecting *your* interests.

Make sure you have the authority to do what you want to do for the customer. In customer-centric companies, people on the line are given the authority to do things that only come with a supervisor's okay in other companies. Your company may be in the latter category and you need to deal with what is, not what you'd like it to be.

If you do have the authority, ask yourself whether your decision is based on what's right for the customer or what's right for you or the company. Sometimes those things clash and sometimes it's a thin line. But I'm a big believer in the medical credo "First, do no harm." Ask yourself if you will harm anything if you do something unique for the customer. If there's no harm to you, the company or the customer, then do it.

We're not saying to "give away the store." As a kid from a retail family, I learned early on that there was only so much you can do before you start eating up your entire margin. Grandpa could take back the pants for that one guy but he couldn't take back everybody's pants. On the other hand, if everybody is returning pants, there must be a defect in the pants. You're not doing yourself or your customers any good if you continue to sell defective products ... or systems.

Every company has internal issues. The smart ones compile information on those issues and use the information to fix them. There are consequences if you don't fix the issues. But they're *your* issues, not the customer's. You are the customer's advocate.

It's not hard to do. It's not hard to see the world through your customer's eyes.

It's not rocket service.

Rocket Review

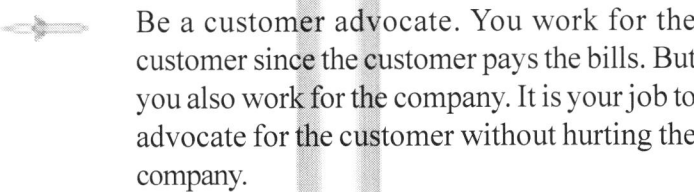

- Be a customer advocate. You work for the customer since the customer pays the bills. But you also work for the company. It is your job to advocate for the customer without hurting the company.

- Trust customers to handle the truth. Customers may not like the truth but they can handle it.

- Don't make customers do unnecessary work. Don't keep them on the phone while you fix a mistake that is *clearly* a mistake.

- Underpromise and overdeliver, but be careful you're not under-promising too much.

- Try to become a "customer hero."

Manager Lift-Off

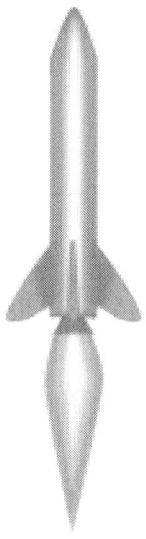

What are you doing to make sure your people become customer advocates? Are you giving them the authority to take care of the customer the way the customer wants to be helped? What are your people doing to show customers they are on their side?

When I spoke to Dan Nelson at AT&T, I told him that I teach people to take the customer's problem and make it their own, to carry the ball for the customer so that the customer doesn't have to fight to make it right. I said, "A true customer hero takes my problem and doesn't let go until it's fixed. Will you be my hero?" He said yes and did what he needed to do.

Dan Nelson was a supervisor. I'm not really sure whether any of his people had the power to become the customer's advocate. In most companies, the CSR is criticized or disciplined for staying on the phone too long with the customer. Here are some things you can do to create customer advocacy:

 Constantly preach customer advocacy. Bring in customer service training that addresses being on the customer's side. Remember what we said earlier: the customer is the most important person in the conversation.

 Reward employees who tell you where your company's actions or policies don't jibe with your professed belief in customer advocacy. Many managers talk a lot about customer advocacy, but when push comes to shove, they establish rules or behave in such a way that says they don't believe in it. Oddly enough, the manager often doesn't realize he is doing it. Allow your people to show you that you are not in sync with what you're saying and reward them for it.

Customer experience guru Lior Arussy asks his clients, "Do you have pictures of your customers on the wall?" It's a great question. Put a face behind the voice or the email. Most call centers and customer centers I have visited are fairly sterile. In the call center, the center of attention is the big board that tells how many callers are in queue and the average hold time. Which would you think is more important? The board or the customer? What if customer pictures were all over your walls, making those pictures a center of attention like the big board is? If you can see your customers, it makes them so much more human.

Make going the extra mile for the customer a major part of your rewards and recognition program. What's that? You don't have a rewards and recognition program? Start one ... now. If one of your people becomes a Dan Nelson, Customer Service Hero, make a very big deal out of it.

COUNTDOWN:

Explain Yourself

The art of explaining is truly an art. You may think it is easy to explain something, but so few people do it really well. Have you had any of the following experiences?

- You ask a friend to tell you what happened at a party where a mutual acquaintance got in trouble. Your friend tells you the whole story and includes every single little detail. Her explanation takes 20 minutes when all you wanted to know was the basics.

- You talk to a technical help desk representative about a problem with your laptop. He explains your problem in such technical terms that you are utterly confused, so your mind starts wandering to what you want for dinner.

- You bring your car in for service. When the mechanic fixes the noise that you'd been hearing for months, he explains what he did by saying, "It was the catalytic converter and I fixed it" but doesn't tell you what was wrong with it. You're intimidated and don't ask because he knows more about cars than you do.

- Your boss makes a decision that will impact not only your time and work but also the whole direction of the company. When you ask why, she says, "Because that's my decision." When you press her, she says, "You don't need to know my reasons. It's my decision to make, and I made it."

- Your insurance company raises its rates without explaining the reason for the increase. When you call customer service to ask why, the representative tells you, "Our costs have risen so we raised premiums." You want more information but the rep says she doesn't have that information and her supervisor is not currently available.

- You return a pair of earrings to a department store. The counterperson says the store doesn't accept returns on earrings that have been worn. When you ask why, she says, "It's the policy."

All of these explanations have the potential to drive people up a wall. If you've been on the other side of these, you know what I mean. We give explanations that are too long, too short, carry too much information, give too little information or use words and expressions guaranteed to anger customers.

CONVERSATION KILLERS

Why would anybody who deals with customers want to get into a battle with them? I constantly see service providers and businesses get into conflict with their customers when they don't have to.

One of the things they do is use what I call "Conversation Killers." I've been teaching these for years in my business writing program, but they have the same effect in verbal communication.

Conversation Killers are phrases and expressions you should avoid when discussing an issue with a customer. Here are some examples of Conversation Killers:

"It is unreasonable to expect …"

"You are wrong ..."

"You are wrong about that / You are wrong in thinking that …"

"You don't understand …"

"Surely you must have known …"

"You failed to …"

"You neglected to …"

"You should have …"

"No, I don't know ..."

"It's not my job …"

"The only thing we can do is …"

These expressions are Conversation Killers because they stop conversations right in their tracks and kill them before an issue can be resolved. The customer has come to us, whether in person, by phone, by email or by chat, and we turned the conversation around by using accusatory phrases and just plain, "I can't do anything" phrases. Let's look at these.

"It is unreasonable to expect …" When using this phrase, you might as well be saying "What makes you think that I would do that for you?" followed by rolling your eyes. In other words, any reasonable person would never ask you to do such a thing. It's better to say instead, *"That would be difficult to do. However …"*

"You are wrong …" When somebody tells you "You are wrong," what's your first reaction? Probably 99 out of 100 customers will take offense. The one who wouldn't either has no self-esteem or is afraid of his own shadow. It's better to say, *"This may not be the case. Let me explain..."*

"You don't understand …" *"Surely you must have known …"* With these phrases, we might as well be saying, "This is very simple to me. You clearly don't have the mental capacity to figure this out." Put

the onus on you, not the customer, and instead say, "*I probably haven't explained myself well...*"

"*You failed to ...*" "*You neglected to ...*" or "*You should have ...*" I don't know about you, but I got tired of people telling me what I had done wrong while I was still a teenager. Whether serving external or internal customers, it's a bad idea to accuse them of being neglectful or having failed. Whether the customer screws up really doesn't matter. What matters is that you take care of the customer and resolve the situation. So instead, say, "*This didn't turn out the way I wanted it. Let's talk about how we can fix it / make it better next time...*" This is especially important in dealing with internal customers.

"*No, I don't know...*" or "*It's not my job...*" This doesn't help the customer. If you don't know the answer, find someone who does. If it's not your job, get the person whose job it is to help. Instead say, "*I'm not sure of that information but I can find somebody who does know the answer / who can help you...*"

"*The only thing we can do is ...*" The key word is "only." As I mentioned in Countdown Chapter 7, customers love options. It gives them a feeling of control. When you say, "The only thing we can do is ..." you're telling the customer, "You have no options, there is no way out of this and if you don't like the answer, tough!" Instead, say, "*One thing we can do is ...*"

Conversation Killers like these are absolutely guaranteed to stop conversations or lead them in directions you don't want them to go. The alternative phrases I have mentioned are guaranteed to keep the conversation going, giving you a much better chance of resolving the issue and making the customer happy.

"It's the Policy"

This is the King Kong of the Conversation Killers, the red cape in front of the bull. This is the one that not only makes customers angry, but also causes them to do crazy things they would never imagine themselves doing. If they were to see someone acting like that, they would say, "Can you believe that guy? What's with him?"

In all the conversations I have with people about the customer experience, "It's the policy" is the Conversation Killer that is the most frustrating. "It's the policy" communicates several different things:

- There is no alternative.
- It's the rule and that's final.
- I have no power to help you.
- I'm not going to help you.
- I don't want to help you.
- I'm putting up a wall that you can't get through.
- You can't have what you want.
- You're going away empty handed.
- I don't care.

Often, when I hear someone use this phrase, I immediately think, "Wait a minute ... you're making this up! You just don't want to help me and so you're making up this all-encompassing excuse that I have no way of countering." Then, when my frustration soars, I either blow my top or walk away, never to return.

It doesn't have to be this way. You do not have to say, "It's the policy." Actually, you shouldn't say it at all.

Two Types of Rules

My daughters were born three years and two days apart, one on January 28th and the other one on January 30th. A local restaurant (*not* Carmine's) has a birthday promotion. If you come in on your birthday, your meal is free.

Now, because our daughters' birthdays are on the 28th and the 30th, we usually go out to dinner to celebrate on the 29th. So we called the restaurant and asked if they would honor both birthdays on the 29th, since we wouldn't be coming in on *both* the 28th *and* the 30th. The manager, without missing a beat, said no. When asked why, he said, "That's the policy."

His reasoning was simple: the promotion is for the day of the birthday and if you're not there on your birthday you don't get a free meal. As I like to say, rules are rules. Whether I'm bringing in my four-person family or a party of eight, I'm not getting those meals free because it's not either of their birthdays. Does this make sense to you? If it does, then you're not customer-centric and your customers will go to your competitor at the drop of a hat.

Yes, the restaurant manager was perfectly within his rights not to provide the meals free. But that's not the point. After he made his ruling, guess where we didn't go for the girls' birthday dinner? And guess where we *didn't* go for my birthday or my wife's birthday?

Let's add up the lost business. On my daughters' birthdays, they would have provided two free meals and been paid for two meals. On my birthday, they would have provided one free meal and been paid for three. On my wife's birthday, one free meal and three paid meals. So, three visits, four free meals and at least eight paid meals never happened. Sometimes, my daughters bring a friend, or we go out with several friends. But rules are rules. I also didn't tell other people about this restaurant that will give you a free meal on your birthday. However, I *did* tell others this disappointing story.

There are two types of rules in business: red rules and blue rules. Red rules are those that cannot be broken under any circumstances. They usually have to do with safety, health, legal, ethics and BIG financial. You must have rules to keep everybody safe and healthy. You have to be ethical. If the government says you can't do it, you can't do it. And you need rules so you don't give away the store. Blue rules are ... everything else. You can bend them if it means making the customer happy without costing the company an enormous amount of money. You know which rules in your business are red and which are blue. They're usually pretty obvious.

Food is actually the smallest expense in a restaurant. That's why restaurants give away free meals in two-for-ones and for birthdays. Because that particular restaurant decided not to, it lost a customer who would have visited several times this year ... and next year, too. With businesses – especially restaurants – engaged in an ongoing competitive atmosphere and with customers having more and more ways not to do business with certain places, can you afford to lose even one customer because of ridiculous rules?

EXPLAIN WHY

The restaurant manager's policy apparently had no wiggle room or *he* had no wiggle room. Either way, he couldn't change the rule and wouldn't find a way around it. Most importantly, he used the word "policy" in his explanation.

Here's an exercise for you. You can do this by yourself or in a group from your workplace.

1. Take five minutes and write down as many current company policies as you can.
2. Then, take as long as you need to write down the reason for each policy. If you don't know the reason for the policy, find somebody who does and then write it down.
3. When you've compiled all of your policies and their reasons, take each reason and try to use your own words in explaining it to another person. If the explanation doesn't sound right to you, try it again using different words.
4. Most importantly, the explanation needs to explain why.

Here's the deal. Instead of using the word "policy," tell the customer why. Let me repeat that. Instead of using the word "policy," tell the customer why. People are more apt to accept your explanation if you explain why. It may not happen in every case, but most of the time people will accept your explanation if you tell them why.

When you explain why, you're telling them that this policy addresses a particular issue or issues and that you are not making it up because you don't feel like helping them. If the bicycle advocate in Portland, Oregon knew the hamburger place couldn't let her in the drive-thru because their insurance company said it was a safety hazard, she may not have sent the tweet that reached thousands of people and made her tell her story on talk radio.

Every policy has a reason. If it doesn't have a reason, it shouldn't be a policy. And, as I said in our exercise, if you don't know the reason for the policy, find out. Most policies are developed after much thought and consideration, and most policies actually make sense. There's a good reason for it. Companies don't set out to deny customers what they want and need.

Tell Them What You Can Do

I arrived at the airport in Austin, Texas, having just finished leading a customer service seminar at the University of Texas. I had a 7:30 p.m. flight scheduled to land in Atlanta around 9:15, which would get me home by 10:00. This would give me plenty of time to sleep before I had to drive almost four hours to Columbia, South Carolina, to meet with a client at 11 a.m. the next day.

I expected to grab a quick dinner at the airport and then get some work done during my flight. When I arrived at check-in, they told me my flight had been cancelled. They had rescheduled me on the 8:30 p.m. flight to Dallas and then the 10:08 to Atlanta, which would have had me home at around 1:00 a.m. This meant that I would be driving almost four hours to Columbia on about four hours of sleep. This would not do.

Helpless.

No flight.

No alternative.

Frustrated.

The airline is losing points.

If I didn't teach this stuff, I probably would have become angry and started screaming at the gate agent. But I didn't do any of that. I knew it wouldn't get me anywhere.

Still, I was frustrated and felt helpless. While holding back my anger, I didn't hide my annoyance when I said, "The 8:30 flight to Dallas? That won't get me home until 1 a.m.! That won't do."

"We're very sorry about that. What I can do is get you on the first morning flight to Atlanta."

At least she apologized and didn't focus on my annoyance or take it personally. She immediately switched into "I can" mode.

Instead of keeping the conversation focused on what she couldn't do, which was to get me to Atlanta on a direct flight at 7:30, she immediately moved on to possible solutions. That, in turn, took my mind off the cancelled flight and got me focusing on the alternatives, getting me on the first morning flight to Atlanta.

"The first morning flight?" I asked. "What time does that leave and get in?"

"It leaves at 6:30, which will get you into Atlanta at 8:15."

My mind was racing. "*8:15? That'll be okay. Wait! I have to be at an appointment in Columbia at 11. Damn!*"

"I've got another question for you," I said. "Can you get me from Austin to Columbia, South Carolina tonight? I've got an appointment there in the morning."

She checked the schedule. "What time is your appointment?"

"11 a.m."

"Here's what I can do. I can put you on the 6:30 a.m. flight to Atlanta and then on the 9:12 from Atlanta to Columbia, which will get you there at about 10:05." This could work!

I Can... I Can... I Can

I'll complete this story later because I want to make this point first: The gate agent knew the magic words to calm an upset customer. First, she apologized. Then, before I could stew in my anger, she told me what she could do for me. By saying, "I can" and "here's what I can do," she made sure I knew she was trying to help me solve my dilemma. And I immediately focused on the alternatives and not my anger.

The anger flew away, which was more than my 7:30 flight was doing.

"I can."

"Here's what I can do."

"What I can do is ..."

"Let me tell you what I can do."

Magic words. Never tell customers what you can't do, always tell them what you can do. She couldn't get me on the 7:30 flight because it had been cancelled. I couldn't get what I wanted. I couldn't get what I needed. I felt helpless. However, she immediately calmed me down by saying "I can."

She didn't look at the problem as if it were *rocket service*.

The first step in explaining bad news and saying what you can do is telling the truth. As we discussed earlier, trust customers to handle the truth.

You may not be able to do what the customer wants you to do, but you can always do something.

STAY UNTIL THEY'RE DELIGHTED

After the gate agent told me that she could put me on a flight to Atlanta and then a flight to Columbia, she added that she would arrange for my stay at a hotel and give me meal vouchers for dinner that night and breakfast the next morning. Everything was all set.

Still smiling over my terrific customer service experience, I called my wife to bring her up to date on my travel plans. She responded, "How are you getting home from Columbia?"

Silence.

I needed a return flight from Columbia and had forgotten all about it. So I went back to the gate agent who had helped me and told her I needed a ticket home.

She looked at her computer and said, "I can get you on a flight home to Atlanta for $567." I recoiled at the price.

"$567? But I'm just ending up where I was supposed to end up – in Atlanta."

"Actually, I didn't charge you for the extra leg to Columbia because we originally were going to put you on a connecting flight from Dallas to Atlanta. But that doesn't include the flight home from Columbia. Let me tell you what I can do (she was so good at this). I can get my supervisor (I didn't have to ask) and see if she can get a lower fare."

Two more "I cans" and I had nothing but confidence that my situation would be resolved. The supervisor arrived, played with keys on the computer and said, "The best I can do for you is $404. But you know what? I really don't have the cheapest fares here. You might be able to get a better fare by calling our customer center. Why don't you have some dinner, go back to your hotel and call? In the meantime, you know what I'm going to do for you? I'm going to upgrade your flight from Austin to Atlanta. You won't have to be on standby for first class. You're in."

Okay, so she didn't say, "I can." She said, "You know what I'm going to do for you?" And it made me feel just as good.

I grabbed a quick dinner, and as soon as I got to my hotel, I called the airline's customer center and told the agent about my situation. At first, she said she couldn't get me a fare any lower than $404 either, and I was starting to ponder renting a car in Columbia and driving home. Then she said, "There's one last thing I can try. If you can hold, I can see what I can do."

She put me on hold and I was treated to "Delta is ready when you are" or some other jingle. As long as I was on hold, I knew she was still with me. Because she had said, "I can," I trusted her.

She interrupted the music to tell me that she had connected with the desk she was trying to reach and they had *her* on hold. She asked me to have patience. I said I would.

Ten minutes later, she interrupted the music again to tell me she was still on hold and sounded as annoyed as most of us do when we're put on hold.

Then she said the magic words: "I will not hang up until I resolve this for you. So if I put you back on hold, please know that I am still working on it." She was clearly my advocate.

I said "fine" and listened to some more music. About 15 minutes later, she came back and told me she could get me a ticket for $295 and swore she had done everything she could on my behalf. I didn't doubt that she was telling me the truth because everybody had done so to that point. I accepted the $295 fare and thanked her for all of her help.

She didn't abandon me when it became too much of a hassle for her. She didn't watch the clock and tell me to call back, which would probably mean I would have to explain my problem again. No supervisor pushed her to wrap it up.

She never gave me a chance to become angry because she and the agents before her kept saying "I can." Though I was upset initially, the thought didn't cross my mind again. I never doubted they would do their best for me because they kept telling me so. I felt as if their complete attention was focused on me and nothing was going to change that.

The minute you take the focus away from the customer's problem and put it on what you can do, the customer will begin to calm down.

We begin to lose points with our customers each time they have a problem or can't get what they want. Engaging the customer in a discussion about what you can do will keep you in her good graces for a long time.

BENEFITS, BENEFITS, BENEFITS

So you've told the customer why she couldn't have what she wanted. She's thinking, "Okay, give me one good reason why I should care." That's why you need to try to get a benefit into your explanation if you can, a reason why the explanation should matter to her. Here are some explanations that include a benefit:

➤ A college won't allow students to sign out equipment from the photography studio in the evening. When asked why, the studio employee explains, "We don't allow you to sign out the equipment at night because we are in an area that has a problem with crime. We fear the equipment will not be safe on your journey to your dorm and neither will you if you're carrying expensive equipment. We can't risk you getting into that situation. What I can do is arrange to have somebody here early in the morning before our usual hours if you want to come before classes begin."

➤ When a woman asks the hospital employee for information about her friend's condition, the employee tells her she cannot give her the information. She says, "I'm not allowed to give you this information because of privacy laws. Those laws are on the books so that when you're sick, nobody – not your boss, your bank, your co-workers or anybody else – can get your information without your permission. What I can do is ask your friend if she is willing to fill out a permission form that will allow you to stay on top of her condition."

➤ The library explains that you can't renew your book a third time. When you ask why, the employee says, "We can't allow a book to be out that long because other patrons have already put their names on the hold list. If you were waiting for a book or a CD, it wouldn't be fair to you if somebody was keeping it longer than they should. Then you'd never get to read that best-seller you've wanted to read. What I can do is put you on the hold list and we'll let you know when the book is available again."

Notice how in each of the above situations the service provider used the word "you" when explaining. He put it in personal terms so that the upset customer could know how someone would be affected by such a situation. Then, after saying "you" with the explanation, the service provider followed with the words "I can."

Put it in Words They Understand

It is important to make sure customers can clearly understand your explanation. Speak in their language, and I'm not talking about foreign languages. I'm talking about the way customers understand things. Don't use terms they don't know.

Try to reference something in their lives, their neighborhoods, or the way they've used or are currently using your product or service. For instance, if you're in a technical field, be careful not to talk above the person's understanding. Technical people have a tendency to use acronyms, technical terms, and words the customer doesn't understand. Having worked with several software companies, I have also found that technical explanations tend to be longer than usual.

Try not to use jargon or acronyms, and if you have to use them, explain what the acronyms mean. Acronyms aren't exclusive to technical people. Every industry, service, office, or process has its own. How many of these acronyms do you understand?

ACE-V, ABR, EC/C3, EOB, KOL, LEC, MDS, SEASIA, SOP, TOS

These are all workplace acronyms friends of mine contributed. They swear each one of these is used in their company or profession. Here are the definitions:

ACE-V - Analysis, Comparison, Evaluation-Variation (method used to evaluate latent fingerprints)

ABR – Available Bit Rate

EC/C3 – Electronic Combat/Command, Control & Communications

EOB – Explanation of Benefits

KOL – Key Opinion Leaders

LEC – Local Exchange Carrier

MDS – Managed Document Service

SEASIA – Southeast Asia

SOP – Standard Operating Procedure

TOS – Terms of Service

Stay away from acronyms such as these, especially if there is somebody in the conversation who may not understand them. Think of it like swearing in a conversation when there's a child present. You stifle the word. Do the same with acronyms.

(By the way, acronyms are much easier to use in emails or any kind of writing. When you use the acronym, put the definition next to it in parentheses. This is called, "a first reference." After the "first reference," you can use the acronym as many times as you want because the reader can refer back to the earlier mention.)

KEEP IT SIMPLE

Keep your explanations short but not so short that you're not giving the customer any information. Customers are sometimes intimidated by those who know more about a particular subject than they do. Therefore, they won't ask questions for fear they'll be considered ignorant.

A young participant in one of my seminars at a technical company said, "Steve, you have to understand something about many of our customers. They're stupid."

Taken aback, I said, "What?"

"Our customers are really stupid. They ask the stupidest questions!"

I looked at the rest of the class to see whether they agreed. Then I said, "Our customers are not stupid. They just don't know what you know. And you know what? You don't know what *they* know!"

Customers deserve respect no matter how much they do or don't know about your product or service.

It's not rocket service.

Keep it simple. Are there people for whom a long explanation is necessary? Of course there are. If you've ever taken one of those personality/communication style tests, one of the categories addresses the person who needs to know *every* detail. If you know that this person needs every detail, give him every detail because if you don't, he's going to ask you for them anyway!

Are there people for whom a short answer like "It's fixed" or "I took care of it" is enough? Sure there are. But in order for this answer to be enough, there must be lots of trust between the two people. If I trust you, really trust you, you can tell me anything and I'll be alright with it. When I lived in New York, my next-door neighbor was a car mechanic. If there was something wrong with my car, he would take it to his garage in the morning. He'd check it out, fix it and bring it back to me at night. (Is that cool or what?) He and I were good friends, and my little girls were at his house all the time. I trusted him with my kids. Why wouldn't I trust him with my car? So when Mike brought my car back and said, "It's fixed," I believed him. And when he told me it was $256, I paid it.

When trying to figure out whether to use long explanations, short explanations, or something in between, know your audience. That should give you the answer.

What if the Customer Doesn't Like the Reason?

I was working with a watch company. After our classes, I told the customer service director to call me any time with questions about customer service situations that came up.

Shirley called me one day and said that she had done exactly what I had told her. She avoided saying "policy" and instead gave the customer the reason. However, he didn't accept the reason and she wanted to know if there was anything else she could have done.

At this company, when a watch needs to be repaired, the owner has two choices. He can go to a local authorized dealer (jewelry store) that sells this watch or send it directly to the company. Bringing it to another watch repair place would void the warrantee.

The problem occurred when the owner chose to send the watch directly to the company. The customer service rep told him the repair department did not accept credit cards and that the customer would need to send a check with the watch. The customer wanted to know why he couldn't use a credit card. The CSR answered, "They just don't take credit cards." At this point, the customer asked to talk to a supervisor and Shirley took the call.

Shirley explained that because the company gets most of their repairs through the stores, the number of direct repairs doesn't justify the money the credit card company would charge them. She ended the explanation by saying "If you use a credit card at the store, it will cost you more, but you are paying for the convenience of being able to drop off and pick up your watch. If we took credit cards, we would have to charge you more, too, and you wouldn't have the convenience I just mentioned." Not only did he not buy her reason, but he also promised never to buy one of their watches again. That's when she called me.

"I believe your reason is a good one," I said. "But that doesn't change the fact that most people expect to pay for repairs with their credit cards, and as we said in the class, expectations are everything. People will decide whether they want to continue to do business with you based on whether you met, exceeded or didn't meet their expectations.

"In the end, every decision a company makes regarding its policies and procedures has consequences, good or bad. You may be perfectly right in your reason but the customer didn't think so. In his view, you weren't being customer-centric. Your reason said to him that you cared more about what the company did or did not spend on credit card fees than making it convenient for him – the customer.

"So, the company has to make a decision: Will I lose more money by disappointing a certain amount of customers than I will by having to pay credit card fees? Your company apparently decided they would lose more money if they did the latter. That's perfectly okay, but the customer was still unhappy."

The company might have decided to charge more for the repairs in general to make up for the cost of using the card. But that may have made other customers unhappy.

Every organization has to strike a balance between making the customer happy and not giving away the store. Sometimes, the reason for the policy is valid and will hurt the company if you don't enforce it. You can't make every customer happy all the time. However, you want to limit the number of people who fall into that category.

It's All About Communicating

The only reason customers get upset is because they feel helpless. The way to overcome that feeling of helplessness begins with communication. When it comes to calming people down, the way you explain can make or break the conversation and make or break the customer relationship. Customer happiness often comes down to the conversation between two people – you and the customer.

It's not rocket service.

Rocket Review

- Be careful of "Conversation Killers." These expressions cause customers to shut down, become angry or ask to speak with a supervisor.

- There are two types of rules: red rules and blue rules. Red rules can't be broken under any circumstances. Blue rules can be bent.

- Avoid "policy." Instead of using "policy" as an explanation, tell customers why. People are more apt to be understanding if you explain why. Try to include a benefit for the customer in your explanation. After you do that, add an "I can."

- Say "I can" as often as possible. The minute you say, "I can" you move the customer away from the problem and on to the solution.

- Be sure to speak in words customers understand.

- Every decision has consequences.

Manager Lift-Off

How often do you practice explaining things with your people? Do they even know the reasons for certain policies? Here are a couple of things you can do:

1. Make a list of all the policies and rules you have that relate to customers (external or internal). Then write down the reason for each of them. Ask yourself if those reasons are important to you and the company and/or if they serve the customer in any way. If you had to explain the reason to the customer, would he say, "So what? How does that help me?" Are these red rules or blue? If they're blue rules, under what circumstances are you willing to bend them? If you don't bend them, what are the consequences to the company? Finally, do your people know the reasons for all of these policies and rules? How well can they explain them to customers?

2. After you've made this list, put together a pamphlet or booklet (or put a page on your intranet) that lists each policy and its reason. Make sure each employee has a copy and can explain each policy and its reason. Many companies inform employees about the rules but don't tell them why they're in place. If people don't know why, they either give the wrong reasons (like, "It's the policy!") or frustrate the customer so much that she asks to speak to a supervisor. Then the problem falls into your lap and you blame the employee for not being able to handle the customer. Employees need to know the rules, the reasons, and under what circumstances they can bend the rules.

A manager complained to me that her people escalate calls too quickly. Then she told me the company's answer to this problem is to have the employee tell the customer that the supervisor is not available, an action guaranteed to make the customer even angrier. A friend said he was told to send a letter to the supervisor, who was in another state, and the supervisor would call him within 10 days. My friend said, "Blood shot out of my ears."

People who deal with customers must have the tools to take care of the question or the problem without having to go to their supervisor. In order to do that, they need to know the reasons for the rules and policies. They must have the authority to tell customers when it's a red rule and determine whether they should bend the rule if it's a blue one. Sadly, managers are often very reluctant to give their people this type of authority.

If you want them to take care of the customer without having to bring you into the picture, give them the authority to make the decisions they need to make.

COUNTDOWN: 2

E-Versations

Much of what we've been talking about up to this point addresses how we talk to the customer face-to-face or by phone. But as I'm sure you've noticed, we are communicating with each other more and more through email, chat, and even social media. One company I worked with informed me that 60% of their interactions with customers now take place through the written word.

Sadly, many people feel insecure about their ability to write clearly, and their correspondence certainly reflects that insecurity. However, writing *is not rocket service* either. It can be easy if you're willing to give it a chance. So let's talk about the written word and the effect it has on customer service, customer happiness and your ability to work with your customers.

WRITING IS THE SAME AS TALKING

Almost all of the customer service lessons we have learned over the years involve talking – what you say, how you say it, what tone of voice you use, etc. Few, if any, customer service courses include writing and practicing writing. It seems as though customer service communication is stuck in the time before papyrus.

So, after years of taking customer service courses, we still have no idea how to communicate with customers through the written word. But here's the good news: writing can be as easy as talking.

It's not rocket service.

What's that? Your 10th grade English teacher told you not to write like you talk? And she told you writing, especially business writing, is much more formal? And in the workplace, I'll bet somebody along the line has said you can't communicate with customers in emails like you talk to your buddy on the playground.

Well, your teacher was right ... and wrong. Writing for business is not Shakespearean, and it has changed significantly over time. Writing and language evolve. What was true even 15 years ago may not still be true today.

You wouldn't talk with customers on the phone or in person like you talk with your buddy on the playground. This also holds true when sending correspondence. You would never call a customer and say "Yo, Dave. What's shakin'?" even if you knew him well. He's your customer, not your buddy. Only in rare occasions will your relationship be that informal with any customer.

So don't worry about it. We can accept that rule because we accept it all the time, and not just in correspondence. You can begin by writing the same way you would speak in a business environment.

BEFORE EMAIL

Since most written correspondence today is through email, let's begin there. It's hard to imagine now, but external email only became a major player in the business world in the late 1990s. Prior to that, companies used email only internally because not every company had an external email system. Even when companies installed email systems, many people, including top leaders, still corresponded the old way because they were more comfortable doing so. Even as late as 1999, many top executives had their administrative assistants type their letters.

I taught a business writing course at several organizations beginning in 1996. The first several years I was teaching that course, I barely mentioned email. People simply did not use email at work, especially when writing to a customer about a problem. So I taught the two most common business writing formats – letters and memos.

Letters are formal and were written in a specific format – date, address, greeting, body of the letter, closing, and signature. The date and address went at the top and the greeting usually started with "Dear" and ended with a colon, not a comma. The body of the letter would be written in formal language, with such expressions and words as, "As per", "forthwith", "party of the first part" etc. (etc. appeared a lot, too). These were not words people used in actual conversation.

Closings included "sincerely," "cordially", "regards" (or "best regards") and "I remain." (I never quite understood "I remain." Was the reader supposed to be relieved that the writer hadn't changed his name since the last time they interacted?)

Letters were used for external communications and only went to people outside of the company.

Memos were more informal.

The language was a little more laid back and often friendly. Memos usually included a few lines or a quick thought.

You often wrote a memo on "memo paper". The memo paper was smaller than stationery and was often pre-printed with "To", "From", "Subject" or "Re:" on the top of the page. This eliminated the need for a greeting.

Closings and signatures were optional. Memos were used only internally, and if you did need to correspond with an external customer, you sent a letter.

THE NATURE OF EMAILS

By their nature, emails are memos. They follow the memo format with the To-From-Subject heading. We write emails with a little less formality than we used to write letters. We often use them to send quick thoughts. Many people don't use closings and even fewer use greetings.

However, we use emails for internal *and* external correspondence, which causes a problem. All of the characteristics of memos go against the characteristics that made letters the correspondence of choice for external communication.

You can almost hear the nervous breakdowns of writing teachers all over the world.

What to do? What to do?

Even as we increasingly use text messaging, 140-character messages on Twitter and status updates on Facebook, we still need a format for general correspondence. Right now, email is it. When was the last time you received a letter from a business that wasn't an advertisement or a legal document asking for money? Emails are here to stay.

Business emails, unlike personal emails, need to be a hybrid of the old letter and the memo formats. Despite the To-From-Subject heading, a business email – internal or external – should still include a greeting.

Now, you don't have to say "Dear." Personally, I'm glad "Dear" is falling to the wayside. "Dear" is a term of endearment or affection. When I write a close friend or relative, my mother, or the love of my life, I'll use "Dear." If I'm sending some marketing materials to a potential client whom I've never met, do I really want to use a term of affection ("Dear prospective customer, I love you")? No dear, "Dear" is not necessary.

Instead, you can begin your email with "Hi Bob", "Hey", "Bob", or "Mr. Jones." It's a lot better than "Dear." By saying a person's name, you are accomplishing the same thing as using her name in a face-to-face or phone conversation. You make the interaction personal and communicate that the customer is a person and not an account number, a co-pay, or the total of her purchases.

Just because it's an email doesn't mean that grammatical rules have gone out the window. You are still required to use proper grammar and accurate spelling in your message. Try to use complete sentences and complete paragraphs as well. I get too many long, one-paragraph emails. And I take one look at an email like that and decide to read it later, if I read it at all. Long, one-paragraph emails lack "white space," and readers love "white space." Whether you're reading a book, an email or a marketing piece, you will be more apt to read the entire thing if there is an abundance of "white space."

An email is not a text message. One client showed me this series of emails:

First email from John: Will I see you at the meeting?

Return email from Paul: Yeah, probably.

Return email from John: Planning on getting there early?

Return email from Paul: I'll be there early if they have donuts.

Return email from John: I'm bringing the donuts.

Return email from Paul: Good. Then I'll be there. Early.

If you're going to have a conversation like this, pick up the phone! I'm amazed by the number of back and forth conversations like the one above that take place over email. They could take half the time and be more productive if the two parties actually spoke to each other. What made this conversation even less effective was John and Paul worked in the same office, two cubicles apart! Either John or Paul could have gotten up from his seat and walked over to the other cubicle. John later told me that he didn't walk over to Paul's cubicle because he didn't want his boss to think he was goofing off.

It's not rocket service.

If you have to exchange more than two emails each way, pick up the phone, arrange to meet with the person face-to-face, or text the person if you have the capability.

DON'T LOOK LIKE AN IDIOT

Recently, somebody told me spelling and proper punctuation no longer count because of the speedy nature of the Web and the tendency for people to use acronyms and abbreviations on Facebook,

Twitter, and other social media. I don't buy it.

When a person doesn't know whether to use "there", "they're" or "their" or use correct spelling, people begin to doubt that person's intelligence. English is a terribly difficult language, especially when it comes to spelling. There are few spelling rules in English that are true all the time. This is because English is a language with many parents. Much of it has roots in Latin (and the descendent romance languages, especially French) but it also features many words from the German and northern European languages. And American English is even worse, carrying with it the influence of centuries of immigrants. But this is no excuse for poor spelling.

I can almost accept bad spelling if you have a non-business relationship with me, but I can never accept poor spelling in business emails. You don't want to lose business because you didn't know which witch is which, whether weather is the right word, or if the lawyer hoped to affect or effect the jury's decision. In other words, people will think you're an idiot if you don't know how to spell or can't use proper punctuation and grammar. Don't give them the opportunity to make that assumption.

Likewise, if you want to use BTW, LOL, ROTFL, or other such chat speak in email, make sure your email recipient knows you well and expects you to use such words and acronyms. Don't assume that you can be casual in your writing just because you had a pleasant meeting with a potential client and the two of you hit it off.

The same goes for tone of voice in writing. People tend to compose emails as if they are talking to the recipient, which is understandable. The biggest problem with email, however, is that there are no vocal inflections, no subtleties, no cues. Your reader can't tell if you are joking or serious or sarcastic, if you are raising your eyebrows, or if you're flirting. Was your comment about the company president in jest? Did you say something with affection or disdain? In face-to-face conversations, they can tell. But in written communication, they can't.

In casual email writing, people use those shortcuts mentioned above as well as emoticons: smiley faces, winks, and sad faces. If it were up to me, I would tell people to use the smiley faces because at least your reader will know you were joking or being cute. However, most people don't expect you to use emoticons in your business correspondence. But this is changing.

Yet although people are not using smiley faces, they are using an awful lot of exclamation points to indicate tone. When I learned how to write, I was told to avoid using exclamation points, but now I see them everywhere!!!!! People are going to find a way to show the tone of their voice, whether by using !!!!!, *italics*, **bold**, or ☺.

THE SAME SKILLS APPLY

Many of the verbal skills we learned earlier in the book also apply to emails and chats.

When replying to a customer request or problem in email, use expressions like "I'll be happy to take care of that for you." As we said when discussing the verbal version of this, you are still answering the unspoken customer question "Are you going to help me?"

Just as you would say your name and use the customer's name in a conversation, you should do the same in an email. It's nice to repeat the customer's name more than once during the message as well. If possible, state your name at the beginning of the message and make sure to include your name in the closing.

If the customer is upset, use the empathy statement we talked about in Countdown Chapter 6 – "I can see how frustrating it can be when your order is not delivered on time" – or some other variation.

And when asking questions, lead into your question the same way as you would in a conversation – "Let me ask you a question about that" or "I have several questions for you. First, what are you ..." If you have more than a couple of questions to ask in the email, say, "I have three questions for you" and then list them. Don't put more than two questions in a paragraph; it seems like an interrogation.

When asking questions in conversation, you usually ask them one at a time and wait for a response. This is not possible in email. And you're not going to send three separate emails with three different questions. So it's important that the questions are numbered or listed in bullets so the reader can easily see each question. If your questions have a particular order, importance or action, use numbers. If there is no particular order, use bullets. When the reader sees the numbers 1, 2, and 3, he tends to prioritize the first question as more important or urgent than the second one and so on.

When someone responds to your questions with an explanation or gives you a long explanation in the initial email, summarize what she said in your response. As we mentioned earlier, repeating what customers say in a conversation lets them know you are completely aware of their situation.

When explaining, lead into your explanation just as you would a question. Explain simply and completely and be sure to explain why. One of the great advantages to email is that you can send much longer explanations. Make sure, though, that you put the most important information up front. If your reader wants more information, he'll keep reading. Remember that most people will stop reading after they've gotten the information they need.

It's also important to check for acceptance after you've explained. Give the reader an opportunity to respond if he doesn't agree with or accept your explanation.

A good shortcut when responding to questions in an email is to put your answers next to the original question in a different color. This way, the reader can see your answer in the context of what she asked without having to refer back to the original email below. If you're not going to use this technique, make sure you refer to the original question when replying, especially if the reply is coming in more than an hour later. I may not remember what I asked by the time your reply comes.

An editor once told me, "90% of your readers will read your first line, 85% will read your second line, 80% will read your third line, 75% will read your fourth and it drops significantly from there. If you want your reader to notice something, put it in the first two lines." Don't spend too much time on idle email chatter.

Putting it Together

There are three simple steps when it comes to any kind of writing: pre-writing, free-writing, and re-writing.

Pre-writing is what you do before you write. This is when you prepare, do your research, gather your information, and have everything at your fingertips. You may think that pre-writing is not necessary in most emails because they're not long reports or papers. However, some of the biggest email mistakes happen when the writer hasn't had all the information he needed, even on a small scale. You wouldn't respond to a request for a meeting without checking your calendar, would you?

Free-writing is what you do when you write. Sit down at your computer or with your Blackberry and simply write your email or other document. Just write. Don't worry about how good it is or how easy it is to read. Don't worry about grammar. The name of the game here is to get your ideas down. Even if you're incredibly angry, just write. Don't worry about the words or the tone. Just write.

Finally, re-writing is where the real writing takes place. You've gathered your information and written what you wanted to say, even if it wasn't written well. This is the stage where you fix it – fix the spelling; fix the grammar; take out extra information and extra words. Running "grammar check" or "spell check" is a good idea (but don't depend exclusively on spell check to find spelling errors. It catches most but not all spelling errors). Most importantly, edit out anything that can be offensive, upsetting or sound angry. This is where you ask yourself, "Do I *really* want to say that? Do I *really* want her to read that?"

This third step is extremely important when writing emails or texts. We tend to write emails at the speed of conversation and don't check what we're actually saying. When we do this, it can be catastrophic.

Writing is Forever

My mother always told me, "If you don't want somebody to see it, don't put it in writing. If you say something about someone or something, you can deny it later or say you were misquoted. If it's on paper, it's permanent."

Email doesn't disappear just because you deleted it. It's on the hard drive somewhere, whether you delete it or not. People have been convicted in court because of emails they thought were gone forever but weren't. As I said before, email is a conversation that's in writing and can be seen by anybody.

We've all heard horror stories of people who sent an email to the wrong person or forwarded an offensive joke or cartoon. Suffice it to say be careful what you write and check your email before you send it. And re-write, re-write, re-write until you've taken out anything that can hurt you later on.

Email and other forms of electronic correspondence are quickly becoming the future of communication. Our kids can type on their keyboards and mobile phones at the speed of light. Some reports already say these young people have problems communicating *without* typing. If you plan on being in the working world for more than the next five years, you better learn the etiquette of writing electronically. And remember, conversation is for now. The written word is forever.

It's not rocket service.

Rocket Review

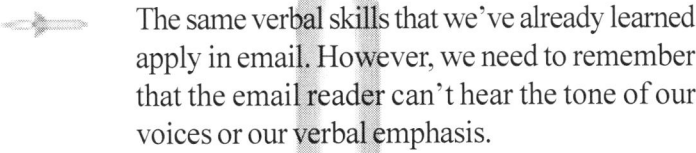

- The same verbal skills that we've already learned apply in email. However, we need to remember that the email reader can't hear the tone of our voices or our verbal emphasis.

- Pre-write, free-write, re-write.

- Emails are memos but they're external. Though we write emails more casually, remember that the external customer is judging you based on this correspondence.

- Spelling and grammar are important even if it seems that spelling and punctuation don't matter in the cyber-world. Still, don't go crazy on the latter: excessive exclamation points can be annoying!!!

- If you exchange more than three emails in a 10-minute period, pick up the phone.

- Be careful: writing is forever.

Manager Lift-Off

As a manager, do you assume your people know how to write properly? If your people are communicating with their external customers through email as many are, are you risking long-term relationships by focusing on their telephone and verbal skills and ignoring their writing training?

The "e" world is fast becoming businesses' favorite form of communication. To use computer terms, we are engaging in e-versations:

Release 1.0 was email.

Release 2.0 was the online chat.

Release 3.0 is social media.

We are leaving our people to figure out the process, the words to use and the etiquette of these three releases without any training or advice from management. We risk major consequences when our people are communicating with customers.

I mentioned earlier in the chapter that I teach business writing. As late as 2000, most business writing focused exclusively on letters, memos, and reports. In 2001, I received my first requests for email training.

Since then, the world of e-versations has only become more complicated. To handle this complicated landscape, most companies have reverted to the forms that made their telephone conversations with customers seem stilted and impersonal: scripts.

I contacted my cable TV company to try to get a problem fixed that had allegedly been fixed three times before. My digital picture was breaking up on occasion, especially during prime time or important sporting events (like the World Series!). The last technician who came to my house to fix it said that if his solution didn't work, the problem was likely a switcher my next-door neighbor was using.

After a summer of light TV watching, the problem started happening again, which told me my next-door neighbor had started watching TV again and using the switcher. This time, however, in an attempt to save time, I decided to talk to someone from the cable company's online chat. "Jerome" came on line to help me. Let's see if you can spot the scripted dialogue.

Jerome: Hello Steve. Thank you for contacting (company) live chat support. My name is Jerome. Please give me one moment to review your information.

(pause)

Jerome: I do apologize hearing this from you and I know where you are coming from. Let me address this concern for you in the best way I can.

(pause)

Jerome: I understand you have a concern on your cable service by having a break picture and the technician visit about this concern as well. I definitely know where you're coming from (Haven't we heard this before?) and I truly apologize for the inconvenience. I ams (that's really what he wrote) determined to resolve your issue and I know we can do this together. I would like to verify how long have you been dealing with this concern, please? If you won't mind me asking.

Actually, I do mind him asking because he did tell me he was taking a moment to review my information. If he reviewed my information, he'd know the answer.

Steve: It's got to be over a year. Have you checked my problem history? Everything should be in there.

Jerome: I am very sorry to hear that this issue happened to you. I can understand the frustration when something is not working the way it is supposed to. I am glad you came to chat. I will do my best to assist you in resolving this issue. Let me check it through the account.

At this point, I've already heard three actual apologies, two "I know where you're coming from" statements and one "I can understand the frustration when something is not working" statement as well as a couple of statements saying he'll do his best to help me. It's been 3-4 minutes already and he still hasn't helped me because 90% of what he has said came from pre-written scripts, which doesn't exactly give me the warm fuzzies.

Then, some more scripts:

Jerome: I am very happy to check this for you. Please allow me two minutes to put you on hold and check this account and get back to you after. Is it okay with you?

Steve: It's fine (considering he told me earlier that he reviewed my account, which apparently he hadn't).

Jerome: Okay. Please allow me two minutes to check this account. By the way, while waiting for your account to pull up, I will share a feature that you can truly benefit from. Do you know that we have Pay Direct?

Because of his scripts, he has now violated the first rule of up-selling and cross-selling – never try to sell the customer something when he's upset and/or you haven't solved the problem yet.

After I said "No, I'm really not interested," he popped in another scripted statement that started with "*Great! I know this will help you a lot*" before proceeding to explain the program.

The chat went on like that for another 15 minutes while he used script after script and didn't solve my problem. Not once did I feel the empathy he had so badly tried to convince me he had at the beginning of the conversation. Finally, I said goodbye, called the customer service line and spoke to a real person who could hear the emotion in my voice and seemed to jettison the scripts.

Here's the thing: customers always know a script as soon as they hear it or see it. They know a script is impersonal, doesn't address the issue, doesn't show empathy, and is created not for their benefit but solely for the benefit of the company. Remember form letters? Those were the scripts we used to send by mail. Customers knew it was a form letter then, too.

If I'm going to talk to a customer service representative or any of your employees, I expect to be treated as a person, not as a situation you can address with a script. If your people are talking to their customers on the phone, you would expect them to speak conversationally. Now, they are increasingly conversing with customers through email and chat. Customers expect the same conversational, non-scripted responses. If you don't think your customers can see that your "chat rep" pressed a key that posted a pre-scripted response on the screen, think again.

Supervisors and companies need to trust their people to say the right things, ask the right questions, give the right answers, and solve the problems without scripts. To do this, these people need to be trained, trained, trained. After training them, test them on their knowledge and ability to solve problems. Then let them do their jobs.

As e-versations become more popular in most cases and the norm in many, your people need training in how to write conversationally and to be more customer-centric in their responses. This is essential as the world of customer communication moves forward.

If you don't trust them, don't hire them. If you hire them, educate them. Throw away the scripts. Train your people. Your customers will appreciate it.

It's not rocket service.

COUNTDOWN:

Exceeding Expectations is Easy

In Countdown Chapter 8, we talked about expectations and covered a number of things:

- Everything in life is expectations.
- Customers have certain expectations and will make judgments about you based on those expectations.
- High expectations = High rewards;
  Low expectations = Low rewards.
- If you meet customers' expectations, you're nothing special. After all, they expected you to.

So, if meeting your customers' expectations makes you nothing special, then what's the point? Whether or not you do what they want, customers still aren't going to be satisfied, right? Yes … and no.

Remember, customer expectations aren't high or low, good or bad, right or wrong. They just *are*. If you want your customers to love you and remain loyal to you, you need to exceed your customers' expectations. Do more than they expect. Go the extra mile or kilometer.

It's Always Worked

The oldest customer service trick in the book is to fix the customer's problem and give her even more than she expected. *It's not rocket service*. Do it a little faster. Make it work better than it ever has. Throw something in that she wasn't expecting. Make the customer forget she was ever upset with you.

I once read a customer service statistic that said 70% of customers with a problem will come back if you solve their problem. Even better, 90% will come back if you solve their problem quickly. Just think how much better the situation will be if you solve the problem quickly and then give the customer something more.

What can you give customers? Let's say you're an equipment manufacturer. Something goes wrong with the equipment you delivered a few weeks ago and the customer is upset or on the verge of being upset. The customer calls and Jennifer, your help desk service person, walks her through a few processes to find out where the problem is. When it turns out there was a manufacturing defect, Jennifer offers to send out a repairperson to fix the equipment.

Most people would stop here. By offering to fix the problem, all you've done is given the customer a chance to like you. What you want is for her to *love* you, to feel she never wants to feel badly about the company again.

How do we make this situation better by doing more than just meeting expectations?

What Jennifer needs to do in this case is to try and think like the customer and anticipate the customer's concerns. If she stops here, the customer may be satisfied but there's an undercurrent of concern. After all, something went wrong with the equipment. The customer is thinking, "So now I have a three-week-old piece of equipment that's already been repaired. What if it breaks down again?" She may not even know she's thinking it, but she is.

So, anticipating this concern, Jennifer offers that she absolutely expects nothing more to go wrong with the equipment after it's fixed.

But to calm any fears the customer may have, Jennifer further offers that if the equipment breaks down again within 60 days, the company will replace the unit (we're assuming Jennifer has the authority to do so or this is an option that is available, though not commonly offered).

Does that make the customer feel love? Maybe. If the customer were on Facebook, her relationship status would have gone from "it's complicated" to "in a relationship." After all, you did deliver a faulty piece of equipment. Love hasn't entered the picture.

Okay, so the machine is fixed. Now, Jennifer sends an automatic email to the client's account manager to alert him of what transpired. The day the equipment is fixed, Scott, the account manager makes it his business to stop by and check things out. The personal appearance impresses the customer, but what really impresses her is that Scott extends the warrantee by a year. This is actually easy for him, because the equipment has a very low repair incident history in general (he also has the authority to do so). The customer is very happy, knowing that even though the equipment is paid for and the warrantee only requires repairing the original three-week-old equipment, Scott and Jennifer went the extra mile. And then, Scott keeps checking-in on more than a regular basis to make sure everything is okay.

Now, your company has more than made up the points you lost earlier from the bad equipment simply by exceeding expectations.

THE BENEFIT OF THE DOUBT

So, about a year later, this same customer has a problem with a different piece of your equipment. It doesn't matter what the problem is – it's a problem.

What do you think happens this time? Do you think she starts looking for another provider? Or might she remember how you went the extra mile for her the last time?

Customers will give you the benefit of the doubt and start the conversation from a place of trust – trust that you'll not only take care of the problem but also that you'll again do the extra things to exceed their expectations. They won't be so willing to jump to conclusions and push you out the door after a positive experience where you went the extra mile.

Was the story a fantasy? Possibly. Can we always do what Jennifer and Scott were able to do? No. But with a world of internet, blogs, and other social media, we've learned that an angry customer can tell thousands about a customer experience within a one-hour period. The statistics show that more people will mention a bad experience than will tell of a good one. Therefore, we have to stimulate the good memories so they outweigh the bad ones.

How do we do this? By giving them something great to remember.

No Problem, Mon!

I won a trip to Jamaica. I entered a drawing when I was at a "Camp Fair" looking for a summer camp for my daughters. About a month later, I received a phone call saying I had won.

I really won! There was no timeshare lecture and no obligation to listen to someone who wanted me to buy something. This was a straight-up winning ticket. Wow!

I had never won anything before so I wasn't sure how it worked. I found out that I actually won two prizes: a resort stay in Jamaica and the airplane tickets to take my family. I had to call the resort to make the reservation and then book the flights.

We received word that we won in early March. My wife and I immediately pulled out our calendar to pick a week for our trip. The kids would be finished with school in early June, so my wife called the resort and booked the second week in June. We would get to Jamaica on a Saturday and come home the next Saturday. The resort was even going to provide us with a nanny for the week so we could spend time alone. This resort had already exceeded my expectations and I wasn't even there yet!

Then she called the airline and told them what date and flight we wanted.

The representative told her that they don't reserve award seats until six weeks before departure. They added that the week we chose probably wouldn't be a problem. After all, the national motto of the island of Jamaica is "No Problem." (This should also be the motto of every customer service department in the world.)

So my wife said, "No problem! I'll call back in a few weeks."

In mid-April, she called the airline and they said they weren't ready to reserve our award seats. They said to call back in early May. When she called back in May, they said call back next week, which would be three weeks before we were to leave.

The airline hadn't really done anything wrong yet, but we were getting a little antsy. Still, our motto was "No problem, Mon! We're going to Jamaica!" We had just begun sipping our imaginary frozen daiquiris when my wife called the airline again. After telling the representative which dates she wanted, this is what transpired:

Agent: I'm sorry, the morning flight on that day is not available.

Arlene: (disbelieving) What?

Agent: That flight is not available. All of the seats are booked. We can put you on the late afternoon flight.

Arlene: Late afternoon flight? That won't work. If we leave in the late afternoon, we won't get there until evening and we'll miss an entire day!

Agent: Well, I'm sorry.

(What happened to "No problem"?)

Arlene: You've *got to* put us on that flight!

Agent: I can't do that. It's completely booked.

Arlene: There aren't four seats?

Agent: Completely booked. I'm sorry.

This was one of those situations where "I'm sorry" just didn't cut it.

Knowing she was about to blow a gasket, my wife handed the phone to me. My job was to find out why we didn't know earlier that the flight was completely booked and to figure out how to fix this situation.

Steve: Let me ask you a question. When did your airline know the flight was full?

Agent: (beginning to become belligerent) I don't know when the flight was booked. All I know is it is a charter.

Steve: A charter?

Agent: Yes, an organization or a travel agency booked the entire plane.

Steve: When did they do this?

Agent: What?

Steve: When did they do this?

Agent: I don't know. Why do you need to know?

Steve: Because my wife first called in March. Then she called again in April. She was told to call back in a few weeks. Then she called a few weeks later. That time, she was told to call next week. And now she called today. The flight is full. If it turns out the flight was completely booked when she first called, why didn't somebody tell us?

(This airline was quickly losing points with me. Considering I'd never flown on this airline before, they were now in the minus column.)

Agent: (more rudely) I don't know when the charter was booked. All I know is that there are no seats. You'll have to go at night.

(I'm officially angry.)

Steve: Well that stinks. We can't change our plans because we already booked the hotel from Saturday to Saturday. So now, we need to miss a day because nobody thought to let us know the flight was booked when we first called. Listen, since you can't help me fix this, I'd like to speak with a supervisor.

And then she said the words that cause so many customers to want to leap through the phone and strangle someone.

Agent: (dripping with sarcasm) She's only going to tell you *what I told you.*

("No problem!" has become "No manners.")

I chose not to blow up and instead firmly asked again for the supervisor. When the agent transferred me – I was amazed she actually did so – I explained our situation to the supervisor. The supervisor treated me a lot better.

Supervisor: (calmly) Yes, I do see that the flight is full. There are no seats. I'm terribly sorry.

Steve: (more calmly) So, what are we going to do now?

Supervisor: Could you hold on a second? I'm going to look at something.

A couple of minutes passed and then she returned.

Supervisor: You said you were leaving on Saturday morning and coming back the next Saturday, correct?

Steve: That's right. It's Saturday to Saturday.

Supervisor: And you don't want to take the later flight because you'll lose a day?

Steve: You've got it.

Supervisor: Let me ask you a question. Could you leave on Sunday and come home the next Sunday? We have room on the Sunday morning flight for your entire family.

Steve: (after a moment of amazement that she was actually trying to help) I suppose I could, but my reservation at the resort is Saturday to Saturday and I'm not sure if they can change it.

Supervisor: No problem. I will call the resort and see if they can change your reservation. Would that be okay?

Steve: Yes!

(I'm beginning to like this airline.)

Supervisor: I'll call you back after I contact the resort. If you don't hear from me within the hour, here's my direct number ...

The supervisor was definitely going the extra mile for me. Fifteen minutes later, she called me back.

Supervisor: I have good news. I've changed your reservation and placed you and your family on the Sunday morning flight. And I apologize for your worry. For your trouble, I will reserve four seats in First Class for you and your family. Will that be okay?

(Her point total not only jumped into the plus column, but she also now has points to spare.)

Our vacation was wonderful. We loved flying First Class where we were served a breakfast that included tropical fruits and croissants.

The airline went from the doghouse to the penthouse in my memory of this incident. The supervisor turned me from an angry customer into a relaxed customer who was happy to tell this story to everyone. (By the way, that airline was Air Jamaica.)

THE PAUSE THAT REFRESHES

I love to tell the story of the employee at one of my utility clients who put his hand in his pocket and spent money to go the extra mile. This employee worked for a natural gas company in the Bayou of Louisiana, where it can get pretty hot on summer days. Sometimes, he told me, the temperature goes up over 105 degrees with extremely high humidity.

The employee, who I'll call Jim, does something special for his customers on those 105+ degree days. When the temperature and humidity hit the high "uncomfortability index," Jim starts his day at his local convenience store. He buys a case of Coca-Cola and a case of Diet Coke and places them in two ice-filled coolers in the back of his truck. Whenever he stops at a house to read a meter or check out a line, he notices if an occupant is standing outside the house. If so, he offers her a cold soda.

Jim explained that these people are his neighbors, literally and figuratively. He thought about how he would feel if he were standing outside his house on one of those days and a utility truck driver offered him a Coke. Jim said he would love that utility company forever if that happened to him.

Jim does this three or four times a summer. He says it costs him less than $100, plus, it makes his customers feel good, it makes them think highly of his employer and frankly, it makes him feel good about himself. Jim truly defines the Golden Rule to "Do unto others as you'd have them do unto you."

It Doesn't Have to Cost Anything

A woman in one of my customer experience classes told of opening her weekly community newspaper and seeing a picture of a co-worker's 8-year-old son shooting a basket in a local park. She smiled, cut out the picture, and delivered it to her co-worker the next day.

This may seem like an elementary gesture, but would you do it? How many times have you seen a friend or acquaintance mentioned in a newspaper and yet don't tear out the article to give to the friend? Recently, an acquaintance of mine was asking around if anybody had a copy of the previous week's "Life" section of the local newspaper because her son's wedding announcement had been published. Several people sheepishly mentioned they had seen the announcement but didn't think to cut it out.

Remember, our co-workers are our customers, too. They deserve the same amount of "exceeding expectations" as external customers do. We can all do things like this for our customers, both internal and external.

It's not rocket service.

Some other thoughts:

- Always think "What else can I do?" or "What do I know that my customer should know?"

- Show interest in their internal situations and time frames. The more you know about your customer's business, the more you can find ways to create these types of golden moments.

- Offer to do the work for them. I'm not saying you should do work that they would normally do, but when you are giving advice, instructions or new ways of doing things, there may be things that are easier for you to do than for them to fight their way through. In my customer service classes, I often give out Starbucks gift cards as prizes. For one class, I asked my client where the nearest Starbucks was so I could pick up the gift cards. She responded, "Oh, don't be silly. I pass a Starbucks on the way to the office. I'll pick them up for you." She went the extra mile even though she was *my* client!

- Be pro-active. You're not being paid to process customers; you are paid to actively serve them. You can always make the most mundane customer interaction an opportunity to do more.

In 1997, the employees of UPS went on strike. When the strike ended, the employees came out ahead in the settlement. One of the reasons was that many UPS clients refused to continue to do business with the carrier in a show of support for the drivers who picked up their packages each day. John Alden, then-vice-chairman of UPS, admitted as much in an August 19, 1997 interview on the PBS Newshour:

"Our customers have always been able to separate our driver from everything else ... if you wanted to favor a corporation or the UPS driver, the UPS driver always wins ... Our customers and the American public have a great appreciation for our drivers."

Think about what it takes to be a UPS driver. At the beginning of the day, he gets his list of deliveries and scheduled pickups. Many, if not most, companies would have a scheduled pickup at the same time each afternoon. All the UPS driver is required to do is stop in each office and take the packages or deliver the packages. He could accomplish this without ever saying a word to the employees at the company, but UPS drivers made it their business to get to know the company employees they interacted with each day. They made a process into a relationship.

When the UPS employees needed someone to stand up for them, their daily clients came through because the clients felt a personal connection to their drivers. Such personal connections come when you do more than expected.

Never Stop Touching Base

The system you put in for your client blew up, crashed, burned, and cost the company time, money, and energy. Your client was not happy.

You sent your people over to fix the problem. You did all the things we've talked about in this book. You empathized; you let him vent. You listened, you acknowledged his pain, and you fixed the problem quickly and completely. You didn't get upset when he got upset. You didn't yell when he yelled. In the end, he let you off the hook.

He even sent you a thank you note for handling the situation.

Your people came back to the office and you licked your wounds. But you were secure in the thought that this customer was still loyal. You forgot all about the problem and moved on.

A couple of years later, you find out through the grapevine that this same client is accepting bids for a new, upgraded system for a new venture. This is news to you because, after all, you're his main supplier of such equipment. Surely, he would have let you know he was looking to put in a new system.

So you call the client. He says, "It's good to hear from you. Been a long time." You ask him how things are going and he says simply, "Fine." There is no appearance of a problem. So you tell him why you called.

"I hear tell you are looking for bids on a system for your new venture. I was wondering why you hadn't let me know about it. Was it an oversight? I'm puzzled."

"No oversight. We just wanted to see what else was out there."

"I understand your wanting to find that out. But we've been your supplier for several years and you didn't contact us," you say, trying to stay friendly and calm.

"Y'know, Bob, you're right. We didn't contact you. Yes, we have been doing business with you for quite some time. But there was that crash last year."

"But we fixed everything. We went the extra mile and you even sent us a thank you note. I thought you were happy."

"We were happy, but then we didn't hear from you. You fixed the system and then there was silence. I would have expected a phone call to ask how things were going. But I heard nothing. We have been a loyal customer in the past, but apparently, you aren't as loyal. I feel you've taken us for granted."

"Why didn't you tell me you were upset with us?"

"I shouldn't have to tell you. If you had called once in a while, you would have known how I was feeling about you. If you want to bid on the new contract, I'll send you the RFP, but let me be honest. I won't give you any points for being our current supplier."

You didn't even know your client was upset. You thought that since you solved the problem there was no problem. You were right…for a while. However, the longer this client didn't hear from you, the more he felt you didn't care.

Doing more than expected and staying on the customer's good side are two different things. If you've ever been in a romantic relationship, you know this!

Your customer was upset with you once. You fixed things and did more than you needed to do. Your job is to do the things that tell the client or customer you're interested in continuing to have a relationship, whether something goes wrong or not.

So, the lesson is follow up with your customer, not only to make sure he's still okay but also that you're still okay with him. Even though you fixed the problem, the feelings that came to the surface still linger. However, there are tons of ways to show your love. (Yes, I said love. If you love the money and the business the customer gives you, you'd better also love the customer.) Just staying in touch reassures the customer that you're still there and willing to do anything to make him happy.

When you've solved a problem, make sure you follow up, sooner rather than later. Offer customers an incentive on their next purchase, or offer to do something that goes the extra mile and shows you still want their business. Apologize again for what happened the last time. Do whatever it takes to let them know they are more than a one-time transaction. And if you're thinking that one lost customer is just one lost customer, think again about all the people they will tell about their bad experience with you.

MAKING UP CAN BE THE BEST PART

One evening, a friend of ours was reflecting on the state of his relationship with his girlfriend. He said, "I heard a speaker say that if you understand that men and women start from different places in their relationships, you can have a relationship in which you never fight. I don't know if I like that idea. One of the best things about fighting is making up. I could make up with my girlfriend for days and it would never get old!"

You and your customers start from different places in your relationships. Like our friend's romantic relationship, you can make the "making up" the best part of your customer connection.

Stay in touch; follow up. Tell your customers constantly that you "love" them, using whatever words and actions you deem necessary.

It doesn't matter where you start with your customers. It only matters where you finish and stay.

You Never Really Know the Customer's Expectations

In Countdown Chapter 8, I recommended that companies and departments should have an ongoing dialogue with customers about their expectations. Customers who understand that relationships are a two-way street will gladly give their providers such information. Armed with a list of customer expectations, it is easy to exceed them.

What happens when a customer doesn't let you know or, better yet, if you fail to update the list of expectations from the ones who did let you know? You won't know how to exceed the expectations. So it is imperative that you're always thinking about how you can make this experience even better and what you would think was special if you were the customer.

Answer those questions and then go out and impress the heck out of your customers. It will result in happier customers, more loyal customers, more revenue, more profit and a happier workplace.

It's not rocket service.

Rocket Review

- If we want customers to love us, we have to exceed expectations.
- Give them more than they expect.
- It doesn't have to be something that costs money.
- Always be thinking about what else you can do. Be proactive.
- That warm, fuzzy feeling will not last forever; follow up.

Manager Lift-Off

In the *Giving Customer Voice More Volume* survey I mentioned in Countdown Chapter 10, 58% of respondents say their companies do not compensate employees or executives based on customer loyalty or satisfaction improvements. That's really too bad.

Many companies and leaders don't do enough to encourage outstanding service in their organization. There is no rewards and recognition program. They don't have a coaching program that teaches managers how to praise. There is no calling attention to how people are going the extra mile. Some managers spend more time catching people doing something wrong than catching them doing something right.

Does anybody know when one of your people goes the extra mile for a customer? Better yet, do *you* know?

What are you doing to encourage your people to do more than is expected? Here are some ideas:

1. Institute some kind of rewards and recognition program. If you're going to give out prizes for outstanding service, make them mean something. I'm not talking about $5 Starbucks cards. When I told this to one manager, he defensively said that they give out several $5 cards per month, but they also give out a "top prize." "Oh, what's the top prize?" I asked. He proudly said, "We double the card value to $10." Oh boy!

2. If you have a rewards and recognition program, be aware that it can become stale for employees. One restaurant I frequent had a plaque on the wall featuring their "Employee of the Month." One December, I noticed they hadn't given out an award since August. The restaurant owner said that after a while, the award had lost its meaning and nobody was getting excited anymore. Change your program from time to time.

3. Make sure that your people feel confident in letting you and others know about what they did for a customer. Most employees don't think it's any big deal. Let them know it is a big deal.

4. Encourage your employees to "reverse-tattle" on their co-workers. Instead of bringing bad behavior to your attention, encourage them to let you know how their co-workers did just a little more than expected. You may not believe it, but most employees are modest about their accomplishments. They need others to promote them.

5. When conducting customer surveys, be specific in asking about things your people did to make them happy. Customers don't usually volunteer such information. You have to ask.

6. As we said in Countdown Chapter 8, you can't exceed customer expectations unless you know what they are. Make finding out about customer expectations an ongoing task. It will determine the company's future and yours.

We Have Lift-Off!

So, are you ready? Are you ready to significantly enhance your customers' experiences with you and your organization? I think you are.

I think you are because I believe you've already begun to use the skills you've been reading about. Any time we learn a new way to do something or begin to understand what motivates people to act in the way they do, we can't help but start to put into action that skill or understanding.

I also believe you're ready because you've always been ready. *It's not rocket service* to understand that most of us begin our interactions with our customers with the best of intentions and that customers do the same in their interactions with us. We *want* to help, we *want* to make things better for our customers and we *want* to receive the compliments and kudos that come with serving people well. We also like how we feel when we know we've helped make it easier for people to work with us, whether they're internal or external customers.

So let's review what we've learned.

Outstanding Customer Experiences are Vital

Year after year, study after study shows that consumers and businesses will go out of their way to do business with companies and stores that give them outstanding experiences. Consumers notice and financially reward companies that deliver superior service. They will make decisions about companies based on the experiences they have had or the experiences others have told them about.

Customer experience is at least as important as what caused the customer to buy in the first place. Sales is responsible for getting the customer in the door and purchasing, but customer service and the experience keeps customers coming back.

Each one of us has the future of our companies and our jobs in our own hands.

It's not rocket service.

Start with a Strong Launch Pad

Customer experiences start at the top and move their way through the organization. Each employee touches the customer experience in some way even if he or she doesn't have direct contact with the customer. A customer-centric environment will help each employee become a customer advocate, dedicated to taking the customer's experience to a higher level.

Employees must have the authority and the knowledge to fix customer issues, be valued, educated, and nurtured, as well as take the responsibility to create great experiences.

Scripts should be used in highly regulated and legal situations and rarely otherwise. Supervisors must make sure their employees know when to use and not to use scripts, and when they have the authority to make decisions and when they don't. This will greatly reduce escalations and create a much smoother experience for the customer.

And finally, you can hire people and try to teach them to be good customer people or you can hire good customer people and teach them the skills they need to be outstanding.

It's not rocket service.

IT'S NOT ABOUT YOU

The more you make the interaction about what the customer wants, needs, desires, and expects, the more the customer will make it about you. When you make the customer the most important person in the conversation, he will appreciate your attention and continue to do business with your company.

When working with a customer, always remember that the goal is to come to a satisfactory conclusion for both the company and the customer – but especially for the customer. It's not about what you want, what you need, what you think is right or wrong. It doesn't matter if the customer yells at you. It's about your ultimate goal – helping the customer.

It's not rocket service.

EXPECTATIONS ARE EVERYTHING

Customers have expectations when they begin their interactions with you, begin their relationships with you, and begin to use your products or services. How you meet or exceed those expectations will determine whether they're happy, sad, thankful, or angry, and it will determine whether they will continue to do business with you.

You can't exceed customer expectations unless you know what they are. One of the biggest mistakes people and companies make is to assume they know what their customers expect. You can't know unless you ask.

Find out what your customers expect from you. Find out what they want. Find out what they need. The more you know the better you can serve them.

It's not rocket service.

Treat Your Customers with R-E-S-P-E-C-T

Customers want you to treat them as individuals with individual wants, needs, and situations. You may have heard the problem hundreds of time, but it's the first time it's happened to them. Show them respect, give them your total attention, let them know what's coming next, give them constant communication, help them feel in control, and reassure them that you care about them and only them at that very moment.

It's not rocket service.

Customers Feel Helpless

The only reason customers ever get upset is because they feel helpless. Somewhere along the line, they decided that you or your company is not going to help them and so they lash out. It may have nothing to do with you at all. You may be the most customer-centric, conscientious employee around, but they're going to lash out anyway.

It doesn't mean they're difficult. It just means that somewhere, somehow something happened that convinced them that they need to fight to get what they want. Show them they don't need to fight by letting them know from the beginning of their experience with you that you feel their pain and you will do everything you can to help them.

It's not rocket service.

It's Not a Game of "Name that Problem"

The art of asking questions is extremely valuable. Even though you've heard the problem 100 times before, it may be different this time. Ask enough questions, both open and closed, to find out what the situation is, what the customer is feeling, and what the customer has experienced so that you can determine the best solution. Don't be so quick to name the problem and assume you know what it is. We all know what happens when we assume. Don't let it happen to you.

The more information you can gather the better you'll be able to help the customer. Don't limit yourself in terms of number of questions, time on the phone, or information you need. The best solutions come from asking more questions.

However, questions can sometimes be perceived as an attack. Make sure you lead into your questions to let the customer know what's coming. The more she knows about the question or the number of questions, the calmer she will be. The calmer she is, the easier it will be for you to solve her problem.

Make sure you know what the real issue is. What you think she's complaining about, and even what she says she's complaining about, may not be what she is really complaining about. Ask questions to get to the bottom of the issue and don't be so quick to say no.

It's not rocket service.

CUSTOMERS NEED ADVOCATES

Let customers know you're on their side. Customers want an advocate. But being an advocate doesn't mean siding with the customer at the expense of the company. We need to find ways to create good outcomes for both the customer and the company.

Customers want you to take their problem, hold it in your hand, and carry it until it's solved. They don't want to be transferred, transferred, transferred, put on hold, or dropped. They want to know that once they tell you about the problem, you will take care of it or find someone else who can. It's the least they should expect.

It's not rocket service.

EXPLAIN "WHY"

If a customer can't get what he wants, has to wait, or has to accept a solution other than the one he was expecting, you'd better explain why. If you explain why, the customer is more apt to go with you. Telling him "it's the policy" or "that is all you can do" sounds like you're making stuff up just so you don't have to deal with his issue. Instead of using the word "policy," tell him why.

There are red rules and blue rules. Red rules cannot be broken under any circumstances whatsoever. They usually have to do with safety, health, legal or big financial. Everything else is a blue rule. Blue rules can be bent for the sake of the customer in certain situations. You and your organization have to determine which rules are red and which are blue. If they're red rules, there better be a good reason for them and employees need to know those reasons so they can explain them to customers.

Customers aren't stupid. Trust them with the truth. When you tell them the truth, they will respect you and believe you respect them. And respected customers are much easier to work with.

Employees don't like dealing with unhappy customers.

Unhappy customers create unhappy employees.

Unhappy employees create unhappy companies.

Unhappy companies create more unhappy employees.

Unhappy employees create unhappy customers.

And the cycle continues.

It's not rocket service.

E-Versations

More and more, people are communicating through the written word – email, text, social media, and chat. Despite popular opinion to the contrary, there is a right way and a wrong way to write emails.

All the skills it takes to make the customer happy can be used in email. Use the customer's name, tell her you'll be happy to help, lead in to your questions and explanations, explain simply, and make her feel like you care.

It's not rocket service.

Exceeding Expectations is Easy

If expectations drive customer happiness, then we are obligated to exceed those expectations. If you do what the customer *expects* you to do, he's not going to put you on a pedestal. Actually, he may not remember you at all. After all, you met his expectations, but hundreds of other customer service specialists can do that as well.

Customers put points in our "experience bank accounts" when they have an experience they enjoy. Meeting expectations may get you a few points just for getting the job done. But if you want to gather up piles of points that will act as a buffer when things go wrong – and something will eventually go wrong – you need to exceed your customers' expectations and surprise them as often as possible.

Give them something to remember you by.

It's not rocket service.

You're Competing with the World

Customers can do business with anybody, anywhere, and they can talk about you with anybody, anywhere. Social media and the Internet have opened up the ability to spread good and bad news about companies and employees. Facebook, Twitter, blogs, consumer comment sites, and just plain old websites are changing the way we talk about our customer service experiences. As I write this, people are developing new and better ways for people to talk about you, your products, and your company. The only way to stay ahead of the game is to provide consistent, outstanding, differentiated customer experiences.

Also, you are not only competing with your competitors. You're competing with every customer experience customers have ever had.

It's not rocket service.

Own the Experience

I was given the task of creating the hospitality area for the National Speakers Association conference in my hometown of Atlanta, GA. This would be the first thing attendees would see when they came to the Marriott Marquis hotel, so it had to be good.

My wife and I went to our local party store to get decorations, and we decided to fill the hospitality area with balloons. We found bags of peach-colored balloons as well as a great peach-shaped balloon with a cartoony face. Since Georgia is the "Peach State," peach-colored and peach-shaped balloons were perfect. We decided that we would place one peach-shaped balloon in the middle of each table with two peach-colored balloons on either side.

Best of all, there would be a large archway by the escalators that said "NSA Georgia Welcomes Y'all." The archway would be covered in balloons. Attendees would be met with a "sea of peach."

The night before the conference would begin, we picked up the helium tank from the party store and drove 35 minutes to the hotel. After dinner, we started decorating.

About 15 minutes after starting the process, we ran out of helium. We had filled about 23 balloons at that point and still had another 65 to go. Clearly, something was wrong with the tank. So I called the party store. A woman answered the phone and I explained the situation. She was not helpful.

Woman: Well, I don't know what to do about that.

Me: So you're not going to help me get another tank?

Woman: (nasty and uncaring) There's nothing I can do! Besides, we're closing shortly.

Me: What if I drove the 35 minutes to get to the store? You can hand me a new tank and I'll be out of there.

Woman: That won't do. We'll be closed by then, and I've got things to do and places to go.

Can you believe she actually said, "I've got things to do and places to go"? After going back and forth with her and even having her call her supervisor at home, she told me my options were to come in the next morning to pick up a new helium tank or do without it. Neither choice was acceptable. I wasn't going to settle for a 23-balloon hospitality area. Frustrated, I hung up the phone and looked for alternatives.

My friend Randy, who was helping with the set-up, suggested I ask the hotel concierge if he knew where I might be able to get more helium. So I called the concierge, and he said, "I don't know if there's any place outside the hotel for you to get helium, especially at this late hour, but I believe the gift shop sells balloons. Maybe they have helium."

The gift shop! Why didn't I think of that?

The Marriott Marquis in downtown Atlanta has three levels besides the guestroom levels. The main level is where guests enter the hotel and register. Downstairs is the ballroom level, which was where we were. Upstairs from the main level is a mezzanine level, which features several stores, including the gift shop.

So I ran up the stairs to the main level and then up the stairs to the mezzanine level. Out of breath, I just about flew into the gift shop. There I found a young woman puttering around behind the counter. She asked how she could help me and I told her my tale of woe.

"How many balloons do you have?" she asked.

"About 65 ..." I answered, with my voice trailing off.

She turned and looked behind her and said, "Well, I've got helium. I don't know how much helium I have, but you can have whatever is in the tank."

WOW! How simple was that? Considering I spent almost 20 minutes on the phone with the woman in the party store and received no satisfaction, this was refreshing.

So I ran down to the ballroom level, grabbed the balloons and

Randy and ran back up to the store. We established a system: Randy and the woman in the store would fill the balloons, I would run the balloons downstairs and hand them to my wife, and my wife would place them on the tables. It was a plan!

So up the stairs I went, grabbing the finished balloons and running them down the stairs, over and over again. At one point, the woman asked me, "Do you need a ladder for anything?" I quickly thought and realized that yes! I needed a ladder to put the balloons on the archway that said, "NSA Georgia Welcomes Y'all." So she gave me her ladder. There was nothing she wouldn't do for me.

Finally, after running up and down and up and down and up and down countless times (I got a lot of exercise that night), Randy handed me a bunch of balloons and said, "That's it."

"That's all the balloons you could fill?" I asked.

"No, that's *all* the balloons," he answered with a smile.

This time I *walked* down the stairs and placed the last balloons on the tables.

I went back up to the store and asked the woman, "How much do I owe you?" She responded, "Oh, just give me a couple of bucks to put in the cash register."

"A couple of bucks??" I asked in astonishment. "You just saved my butt!"

"I sold you *air*," she replied. She was right if you think about it.

"Can't I do *anything* for you? Can I write a letter to your manager?"

"*That* you can do," she answered and handed me a business card with her manager's name on the front. She wrote her name on the back. I thanked her and left.

The next day, Friday morning, people arrived at the conference from all over the U.S. and the world and were met with a "SEA of peach" – peach balloons everywhere. And all weekend everybody talked about the terrific hospitality area.

IT'S NOT ROCKET SERVICE

The morning after the conference, I went into my office and immediately began to write letters. First, I wrote a letter to the woman in the gift shop, thanking her for the enormous help she gave me. Then I wrote a letter to her manager and sent a copy to the hotel's catering manager, with whom I had been working. Then I said, "Hmm ... one more letter."

I wrote a letter to Bill Marriott at Marriott Headquarters to tell him about the wonderful employee he had working at his Atlanta property.

Why did I take the time to write a letter to Bill Marriott? Here's why:

As I was walking out of the gift shop that night, I realized my shoelace was untied. When I bent down to tie my shoelace, I noticed the opening and closing times for the store at the bottom of the glass doors. For that Thursday night, it said, "Closing time: 10:00 P.M." I looked at my watch. It was 11:05. And she never told me.

She never said, "Hey, it's getting late. I've got to go."

She never said, "I can't help you. We're closing soon."

She never said, "I'm sorry, the helium is only for the balloons *we* sell."

All she did was take my problem from me, hold on to it, do what needed to be done to fix it, and stay with me until it was finished. Not only did she exceed my expectations by helping me at all, she exceeded them by keeping her attention focused on me and even going so far as to stay late. She owned my experience.

It doesn't take high intelligence to give of yourself for the sake of your customer.

It doesn't take a special person not to let go until the problem is fixed.

It doesn't take a rocket scientist to figure out what to do with this situation.

It's not rocket service. It's something we all can do, and do well.

Notes

Here are some notes and citations on stories, studies, surveys, and books I mention in the preceding pages.

Readers, please note: Internet Web sites offered as citations and/or sources for further information may have changed or disappeared between the time this was written and when it is read.

INTRODUCTION

- The *2010 Customer Experience Consumer Study* was conducted by Strativity Group, Inc. (www.Strativity.com). Strativity does this survey once a year as well as several others to measure customer attitudes towards the customer experience. A summary report as well as many more interesting reports are downloadable from the website, including one in which a majority of executives say their companies don't deserve its customers' loyalty.

- A very interesting PowerPoint presentation on the *2010 American Express Global Customer Service Barometer* with many more statistics about customer behavior in the face of different experiences is available at home3.americanexpress.com/corp/pc/2010/pdf/CSSurvey_MarketCompare.pdf.

COUNTDOWN CHAPTER 10

- More information on CMO Council and Sabermetrix's *Giving Customer Voice More Volume* study can be downloaded at www.satmetrix.com/resources/research/giving-customer-voice-more-volume-cmo-council.

- To download a complete list of *Training Magazine's* 2011 Top 125, with statistics and reasons why the companies were chosen, go to www.trainingmag.com/article/2011-training-top-125.

- *The Best Service is No Service: How to Liberate Your Customers from Customer Service, Keep Them Happy & Control Costs*, by Bill Price and David Jaffe was published in 2008 by Jossey-Bass. The book is available on Amazon.com in hardcover and Kindle versions. It's a terrific book that takes a few angles I hadn't thought of before.

- The statistic, "68% of customers stop doing business with a company because of the way they were treated, while only 14% stopped because of the product" has been attributed to many different surveys but most often is not attributed at all. This may be a case where a statistic has been passed along and passed along and nobody knows if it's true or not. However, other surveys have shown similar numbers, so I felt okay including it.

COUNTDOWN CHAPTER 8

- The JD Power survey on home appliance retailers noted in the story about Best Buy and hhgregg can be found at jdpower. businessweek. com/Homes/ratings/home-appliance-retailer-ratings.

- The story about the Best Buy employee who found the iPhone tripod on eBay was from "Best Buy investing in 'blue shirt' staff to keep it at the top" by Andria Cheng, *Columbus Dispatch*, October 31, 2010. www.dispatch.com/live/content/business/stories/2010/10/31/best-buy-investing-in-blue-shirt-staff-to-keep-it-at-the-top.html.

- Ken Futch's story about the $10,000 raise is from his great book, *Take Your Best Shot: Turning Situations into Opportunities*, published in 2005 by Wagrub Press. Ken has perfected the art of being a speaker of very important business topics while being one of the funniest men on the planet.

COUNTDOWN CHAPTER 7

- Stephen Covey's "Emotional Bank Accounts" were first mentioned in his landmark book, *Seven Habits of Highly Successful People*, published by Free Press in 1989.

COUNTDOWN CHAPTER 6

- The story of "United Breaks Guitars" and the quotation can be found on Dave Carroll's website www.davecarrollmusic.com/ubg/story. You can find the video on YouTube at www.youtube.com/watch?v=5YGc4zOqozo. You will be about the 10 jillionth person to watch it.

- The American Express Survey is the same as in the book introduction.

- I first learned the three-level empathy statement from Dr. Richard Strand of Customer Focus, Inc. and it is featured in the customer service training program, *Creating CEOs*.

Countdown Chapter 5

Name That Tune originally aired on NBC radio in 1952 and the original TV version of the program aired on both NBC and CBS from 1953-1959. It has reappeared in several different forms starting in the 1970s with the last version ending in 1984. The rights to the show, concept and name are owned by MTV Networks.

The "Echo Technique" story has been around for quite awhile. The first speaker I heard tell it was Jeff Slutsky, whose version was hysterically funny and longer than mine is. Since that time I've heard it attributed to several speakers, including Zig Ziglar. So I don't know who created the original. Jeff, if it was you, I apologize for using your story.

Countdown Chapter 4

The Lior Arussy story about the employee from legal is actually slightly different from the one I told. I recalled it from memory. You can find Lior's original version in his book, *Customer Experience Strategy: The Complete Guide from Innovation to Execution* published in 2010 by 4i, a Strativity Group Media company. If you are looking for what to do next after you read this book and want to make a lasting change in your company's customer experience, this is the book to read. It is available on Amazon.com.

You can look up the Dan Nelson Customer Service Hero blog at my blogsite: www.SteveCohn.ItsNotRocketService.com.

The story about Josh Muszynski and the $23 quadrillion charge was published by the Associated Press, July 15, 2009. I first saw it in USA Today www.usatoday.com/news/nation/2009-07-15-new-hampshire-charge_N.htm. You can see the original statement from Bank of America and meet Josh in a video from local Manchester TV station, WMUR, www.wmur.com/r/20057331/detail.html.

Countdown Chapter 1

The customer service statistic that says 70% of customers with a problem will come back if you solve their problem and 90% will come back if you solve their problem quickly is another one of those customer service statistics that is repeated over and over again and nobody seems to know its origin. However, as with the statistic I noted in the Countdown Chapter 10 notes, there are enough surveys done since that show similar numbers.

- I remember hearing the story of customer loyalty to their UPS drivers at the time of the 1997 strike, and hoped I could find a cite that told me I wasn't imagining it. Thank you Internet. The entire PBS Newshour program segment transcript from August 19, 1997 is available at www.pbs.org/newshour/bb/business/july-dec97/ups_8-19.html.

- Information on the *Giving Customer Voice More Volume* survey is in the notes from Countdown Chapter 10.

About Steve Cohn

Steve Cohn, CSP, helps companies and people create better and more successful relationships with customers, prospects, employees and each other.

Steve lives and breathes customer relationships. He has spent most of his professional career studying the way people communicate with each other and how their actions affect their businesses, their relationships, and their environments. He has found that true, loyal customer relationships can only happen when the person providing the product or service truly focuses on and communicates with the customer.

Steve has extensive experience as a seminar leader and consultant in call center, corporate, and retail customer relations as well as interpersonal and written communication. He has worked with such diverse organizations as FedEx Worldwide, BlueCross BlueShield, Delta Air Lines, IBM, E.ON Energy (UK), Atmos Energy, Lincoln Financial, Mazda, KeyCorp, Thomson-Reuters, the City of Los Angeles, University of Louisville Health System and many others in more than 35 states, seven countries and Puerto Rico.

His incredible speaking ability and rapport with audiences and clients helped him earn the CSP designation – Certified Speaking Professional – from the National Speakers Association in 2002. The Certified Speaking Professional designation is the highest earned designation in the speaking and training business and is held by less than 10% of professional speakers and trainers worldwide.

He began his career as a journalist, working in radio, print, and video for such organizations as NBC, the Associated Press, and United Press International.

Steve is a past-president of NSA-Georgia, a state chapter of the National Speakers Association. He lives with his wife, Arlene in Alpharetta, Georgia, has two grown children, Ariel and Hannah, and grew up in Brooklyn, New York.

Want More?

Like what you read? Now bring Steve Cohn to your company, association or organization.

KEYNOTES AND BREAKOUT SESSIONS

It's Not Rocket Service:
Managing, Meeting and Exceeding Customer Expectations

Designing and delivering outstanding customer experience requires not only feedback from experiences customers have already had but also anticipation of what those customers' expectations are before the experience. Will you lose customers because there's a disconnect between what they really expect and what you *think* they expect? When people can make purchases from anywhere, you need to know, understand and exceed your customers' expectations. In this high-energy presentation, Steve shows you how to create a strategy for determining your key customer expectations and using them to surprise customers and create loyalty.

SEMINARS AND TRAINING

CUSTOMER EXPERIENCE PROGRAMS FOR ALL EMPLOYEES

Creating CEOs: Customer Experience Owners

In an era of commoditized products and mediocre service, employees must do everything they can to own their customers' experiences and make the customer feel like the most important person in the world. In this highly interactive customer service program from Customer Focus, Inc., Steve uses many of the concepts in his book as well as teaches your people valuable interpersonal, customer-friendly skills. Learn how to see the world through your customers' eyes, own the customer's experience from start to finish, and create great customer memories and loyalty to your products and company.

E-Versations

A recent study showed that 65% of executives prefer to receive email more than other forms of communication, up from 34% a decade ago. Because of this, your emails can make or break your relationships with customers, co-workers, and suppliers and can dictate the future of your career or organization. Steve will show you how to create emails and other written communication that connect with the reader, generate action, and keep relationships that are long-lasting and profitable.

Patient's VOICE Skill Clinics (for Healthcare)

Skill Clinics, from Customer Focus, Inc. are 1-hour, on-site manager-led workshops developed in hospitals to meet today's demands for collaborative healthcare. These workshops develop the service skills that raise patient satisfaction scores, improve the teamwork skills shown to reduce errors and rework, and create the patient involvement skills that engage patients and reduce re-admissions. The program also comes with an accountability system that involves employees and their supervisors in a team effort to assure the skills and progress gained from the Clinics continue. With Medicare reducing reimbursements based on hospital HCAHPS scores, this program is a must for any health care organization.

Deliver Amazing Customer Experiences at Every Interaction

Providing great experiences for customers is one of the key challenges facing organizations. Customers expect positive experiences and organizations need to meet these expectations at every touch point to be competitive. In this interactive and inspirational program from Strativity Group, Steve helps participants explore the many factors that lead to a customer experience revolution and teaches employees how to install customer-centric change from within. This is not a soft-skills program, but one that helps employees and managers understand the customer experience and the actions they need to take to make it memorable.

Customer Experience Management Programs

Managing Accountable Performance:
Coaching to Behavior Standards and Performance Goals

How do you improve quality and service? The #1 cause of quality, service, and cost issues is a lack of accountable performance standards and goals. In this program from Customer Focus, Inc. Steve will show you how to empower your managers to implement accountability with every employee for quality, service, and cost-control. Managers practice setting performance standards and goals and learn how to coach employees and keep them accountable in a process that is encouraging, motivating and successful.

Embracing Empowerment:
Inspire Your Employees to Deliver Superior Results

Keeping employees fully engaged is a top challenge every organization faces. Managers claim they empower their employees, yet employees don't feel empowered. Organizations with unengaged employees contend with decreasing productivity and customer goodwill. In this interactive program from Strativity Group, Steve helps participants explore examples of highly engaged performances and the value proposition created through empowered performance. Participants explore new ways to engage employees and remove personal growth inhibitors to help them perform at their highest level every day.

For More Information, Contact:

Steve Cohn, CSP, People To People Learning, Inc.

Email:	SteveCohn@PeopleToPeopleLearning.com
Web:	PeopleToPeopleLearning.com
Blog:	SteveCohn.ItsNotRocketService.com
LinkedIn:	LinkedIn.com/in/SteveCohnCSP
Twitter:	Twitter.com/SteveCohnCSP

Index

A

Abusive Customers 88–90, 103–104, 108, 116
Account Number 9, 49, 67, 70, 78, 170
Acronyms 158–159, 171–172
Advertising 50–51, 52, 54, 86
Advocate 25, 40, 93, 129–143, 156, 202, 205
Air Jamaica 186–190
Airlines 4–5, 18, 86–87, 152–156, 186–190
Alden, John 192
American Express 6, 88
American Express Global Customer Service Barometer 6
Angry Customers 9, 27, 34, 38, 77, 81–109, 112–113, 116, 119, 124, 134, 136, 148, 152–154, 156, 163, 186–190, 203
Apology 9, 99–102, 107, 153, 179–180, 195
Apple 51
Arizona Diamondbacks 83
Arussy, Lior 129, 143
Asking Questions 9, 17, 27 31, 63–64, 93, 104, 112–119, 122–123, 125, 127, 173–174, 181, 204, 206
Associated Press 138
AT&T 131–133, 142
Atlanta Braves 50
Attention (to customer) 45, 63, 67, 70–72, 78, 79, 89, 112–114, 119, 125, 126, 130, 156, 203, 204, 211
Authority 4, 12, 14–15, 18, 24, 26, 40, 140, 142, 165, 202

B

Baker, Stephen 47
Bank of America 138–139
Best Buy 46–47
Best Service is No Service, The 20, 109
Blogs 88, 131, 133, 186, 207
Branding 50, 51–52, 54
Burger King 58

C

Carmine's 1–2, 149
Carroll, Dave, 86–87
Chat 30, 71, 147, 167, 172, 173, 178, 179–181, 206
Chevrolet 51
Choices 66, 76, 105, 160, 209
Closed Questions 116–117, 119, 125
CMO Council 15
Co-workers 3, 10, 14, 22–24, 26, 53, 57, 77, 104, 157, 191, 199
Coaching 16–17, 198
Coca-Cola 2, 190
Cohn, Ariel (daughter) 43–44, 68–69, 82, 149–150
Cohn, Arlene (wife) 58–60, 82, 92, 131–133, 186–190, 208–209
Cohn, Arnold (father) ix, 37, 65
Cohn, Hannah (daughter) 71, 82, 149–150
Cohn, Shirley (mother) 175
Coke 191
Coke Zero 2
Columbus (OH) Dispatch 47
Communication 9, 12, 17–18, 24, 40, 53, 64, 70, 72–75, 78, 87, 146, 149, 162, 167–182, 193–195, 204, 206

Control (customer in) 75–76, 78, 104, 105, 108, 113, 115–116, 148, 204
Conversation (most important person in) 35–38, 39, 40, 91, 113, 114, 130, 142, 203
Conversation Killers 146–148, 163
Covey, Stephen 55
Crazy Eddie 46–47
Cross-selling 180
Customer
   Abusive. *See* Abusive Customers
   Advocate. *See* Advocate
   Angry. *See* Angry Customers
   Centric 3, 9, 12, 17, 26, 130, 140, 150, 161, 182, 202, 204
   Choices. *See* Choices
   Control. *See* Control (customer in)
   Culture 12, 16, 21–22
   Difficult. *See* Difficult Customers
   Dissatisfaction. *See* Dissatisfied Customers
   Environment 11–31, 75, 130, 202
   Experience 3, 4–6, 8, 12, 13, 17, 21, 22, 24, 51, 87, 149, 186, 202, 207
   External. *See* External Customers
   Happiness. *See* Happy Customers
   Hero 9, 131–133, 141, 142–143
   Internal. *See* Internal Customers
   Loyalty. *See* Loyal Customers
   Name 15, 67, 69–70, 78, 79, 91, 170, 173, 206
   Not Always Right 35–38, 39
   Options. *See* Options
   Reassurance. *See* Reassurance
   Relationship Management (CRM) 9
   Satisfaction. *See* Satisfied Customers
   Trust 76, 78, 115, 155, 160, 185
   Upset. *See* Upset Customers
   Voice 15, 198

Customer Experience Consumer Study 5
Customer Focus, Inc. 95

D

Daughters 43–44, 68–69, 71, 82, 149–150
Dell 19
Delta Air Lines 4–5, 152–156
Diet Coke 44, 191
Difficult Customers 28, 76, 81–82, 88–90, 107, 109, 125, 204
Disney 51–52
Dissatisfied Customers 9, 20
Dollar Signs (treating customers as) 67, 69

E

Echo Technique 119–121
Email 74, 133, 143, 147, 159, 167–182, 206
Emoticons 172
Empathy 9, 28, 49, 57, 81, 83, 95–98, 101, 107, 121, 132, 134, 173, 181, 193
Empowerment 3, 221
   See also Authority
Escalations 15, 23, 40, 94, 116, 165, 202
Expectations 9, 41–64, 78, 79, 104, 120, 133, 135–137, 161, 203, 205
   Exceeding 9, 41–42, 44, 47, 50, 52, 57, 58–60, 61, 63, 64, 77, 135, 161, 183–199, 203, 207, 211
   Meeting 42, 44, 49–50, 52, 57, 58–60, 64, 77, 93, 120, 161, 183, 184, 203, 207
   Setting 51, 53, 57, 64, 74, 120, 135
Experience Bank Account 55–57, 61, 207

Index

Explaining 9, 17, 25, 76, 145–165, 174, 181, 206
   Bad News 30, 134–135, 154
   Why 151–152, 163, 164, 205–206
External Customers 13, 22–24, 26, 42, 80, 126, 148, 164, 170, 177, 178, 191

F

Facebook 71, 87, 170, 171, 185, 207
Farmer's Insurance 16
Father. *See* Cohn, Arnold
Flexibility 17, 24, 77, 78, 133
Follow-up 22, 45, 63, 193–195, 197
Form Letters 18, 102, 178, 181
Fortune Magazine 46
Futch, Ken 43

G

Giving Customer Voice More Volume 15, 198
Go the Extra Mile 22, 31, 34, 41, 136, 143, 183, 185–186, 190–191, 192, 194, 198
Golden Rule 191
Google 6
Grammar 30, 170, 172, 175, 177
Grandpa Max *ix*, 37–38, 65, 140

H

Happy Customers 5, 20, 26, 28, 40, 42, 162, 167, 203, 207
Health Insurance Portability & Accountability Act 15
Healthcare 15, 68–69, 76, 98, 105
Helplessness 81–109, 114, 152, 154, 162, 204
Hesitant Words 102
hhgregg 46–47
HIPAA 15
Hiring 2, 27–31, 48, 182, 202

I

"I Can" 152–154, 155, 156, 157, 163

Internal Customers 13, 22–24, 26, 42, 57, 148, 164, 170, 191, 201
Internal Issues 13, 14, 24, 88, 140
iPhone 47
It Begins With You 24–25, 77
It's Not About You 33–40, 90, 93–95, 106, 203

J

Jaffe, David 20
Jamaica 186–190
Jargon 112, 158–159
JD Power and Associates 46

L

Land's End 21
Letters 18, 87, 168–170, 178
   See also Form Letters
Lexus 44–46, 48, 51
Listening 29, 111–112, 113, 119, 121, 193
Loyal Customers 3, 5, 39, 42, 103, 138, 198

M

Mackes, Chad 2
Mac's Men's Shop *ix*, 65
Marriott, Bill 211
Marriott Marquis 208–211
McDonald's 58
Memos 169–170, 177, 178
Microsoft 119
Mother. *See* Cohn, Shirley
Muszynski, Josh 138–139

N

Name that Tune 111
National Speakers Association 208
Nelson, Dan 131–133, 142
New York Mets 83
New York Yankees 83
Nordstrom's 40
NPD Group 47
NSA Georgia 208, 210

O

Open Questions 116–118, 125, 127
Options 75–76, 78, 135, 148, 209

P

Patients 15, 68–69, 76, 98
PBS 192
Points (experience account) 55–57, 88, 152, 156, 185, 188, 190, 194, 207
Policies 40, 88, 99, 142, 146, 148–151, 160–162, 163, 164–165, 206
Ponderosa Steakhouse 58–60
Price, Bill 20, 109
Promises 50, 51, 52–53, 54, 135–137, 141
Publix 21
Punctuation 171–173, 177

Q

Questions. *See* Asking Questions

R

React 30, 43, 54, 90, 92, 103–104, 107, 122
Reassurance 66, 76, 195, 204
Respect 24, 57, 65–80, 89, 159, 204, 206
Respond 29, 36, 38, 70, 74, 99, 103–105, 107, 122, 174
Restaurants 1–2, 149–151
Rewards 142, 183, 198–199
Rocket Science 3, 91
Rocket Scientist 2, 3, 10, 12, 62, 211
Rules (red and blue) 14–15, 149–151, 163, 164, 206

S

Sabermetrix 15
Satisfied Customers 11, 36, 47, 198
Saying "No" 17, 87, 121–124, 205
Scripts 12, 17–18, 26, 40, 178–182, 202

Seven Habits of Highly Successful People 55
Social Media 88, 167, 172, 178, 186, 206, 207
  See also Facebook; Twitter
Sorry 83, 95–96, 97, 100–101, 102, 104, 107
Southwest Airlines 21
Spelling 30, 170, 171–172, 175, 177
Starbucks 51, 55, 192, 198
Start at the Top 8, 12, 13, 21, 202
Strand, Richard 95
Strativity Group 5, 8, 129

T

Taylor Guitars 87
Text Messaging 170, 171, 175, 206
Tiffany 51
Tone of Voice 167, 172–173, 175, 177
Tools 10, 14, 26, 40, 165
Training 16–17, 26, 31, 142, 178, 182
Training Magazine 16
Trust 55
  Customers 134–135, 138, 141, 154, 206
  Employees 12, 126, 181–182
Truth 134–135, 137–138, 141, 154, 156, 206
Twitter 87, 170, 172, 207

U

Underpromise and Overdeliver 135–136
Uniqueness 67–69, 77, 78, 119, 140
United Airlines 86–87
United Continental 86–87
Up-selling 180
UPS 192–193
Upset Customers 9, 34, 49, 76, 77, 81–109, 111, 113, 114, 119, 121, 124, 132, 134, 153, 157, 162, 173, 175, 181, 184, 193–195, 204

V
Visa 139

W
Walmart 51
Wegman's 21
Wendy's 58
Wife. *See* Cohn, Arlene
Word of Mouth 44, 50, 53–54
World Series 83–85, 179
Writing 17–18, 30, 159, 167–182, 206

Y
YouTube 85, 87

Made in the USA
Charleston, SC
16 November 2011